IN HI[M]
... OUR HOPE

Pedro Arrupe S.J.

Irish Messenger Publications
Irish Delegation/International Institute of the Heart of Jesus,

37 Lower Leeson St., Dublin 2.

©English edition 1983
Irish Messenger Publications/
International Institute of the Heart of Jesus.

Translated from the Spanish edition
1982, *En El Solo . . . La Esperanza*
Published by the General Secretariate,
of the Apostleship of Prayer, Rome.

ISBN 0 901335 28 2

Design by Dermot McGuinne

Printed by Irish Printers Ltd, Dublin

ACKNOWLEDGEMENTS

The publishers wish to thank all those who helped with the production of this book and in particular, Mr. A. E. Trinidad, Miss L. Canessa, Miss L. Dudley, Mr. C. Durante, Rev. L. Fitzpatrick, Miss M. Martinez, Mrs. J. Neish, Mrs. J. Robles, Mr. A. Suarez, Miss C. Triay, Mrs. J. Nuñez, Mr. J. Nuñez, Mrs. J. E. Francis. We are also indebted to the Most Revd Eugene J. Cuskelly, M.S.C., D.D., Auxiliary Bishop of Brisbane, for permission to use his translation of Part II, *The Theology of the Heart of Christ*. Our special thanks go to the Loreto Sisters in Gibraltar and Rathfarnham for their generous collaboration.

TABLE OF CONTENTS

FOREWORD

The compilers of this selection of some of Father Arrupe's homilies, addresses and writings on the mystery of the Heart of our Lord deserve our thanks and sincerest congratulations. The original version appeared in Spanish under the title *En el Solo — La Esperanza* and was published by the Directorate of the Apostleship of Prayer at Rome. This English version, published with the Director's kind permission is the result of co-operation between the International Institute of the Heart of Jesus and Irish Messenger Publications. In order to make Father Arrupe's reflections available in English without delay, difficult work had to be done quickly and under pressure. I am immensely grateful to all who co-operated so generously and so competently in this task.

Father Arrupe's reflections are profound, moving and modern. They are also significant and practical. He is very much a contemporary man; a witness to the atomic age with all its possibilities of achievement and progress; an eye-witness in Japan to part of its record of awesome destructiveness. He is also an experienced spiritual leader, being General of the Society of Jesus since May 1965. He has had the responsibility of guiding his brethren during years of change and upheaval in the world and in the Church and of helping them to respond faithfully to the demands of the Vatican Council for renewal in religious life.

The decades of his Generalate may have been exciting but they certainly were not easy years. People who know Father

Arrupe personally will tell you that he does not complain. They speak often of his courage, kindness, spirituality and optimism. He combines within himself great loyalty to the Pope and the Magisterium and to the worthy traditions of the Society of Jesus along with an openness to new movements, a perceptiveness of today's needs and a deep compassion for the anguish of modern man. He is not unaware of human weakness and sinfulness. He knows that plans can fail, experiments go wrong and that even serious deviations may occur. His prayerfulness and courage in suffering and disappointment show the supernatural quality of his hope and have brought inspiration and steadiness to religious and lay people all over the world when times were hard and discouragement a temptation.

Such is the quality and the integrity of the witness quoted in the following pages. He testifies to the importance of devotion to the Heart of Jesus today. His testimony is true and he knows he speaks the truth.

' "Heart of Jesus," ' he tells us, 'is a phrase so rooted in biblical meaning that it is irreplaceable . . . the great novelty of the New Covenant is the love of his Heart and the love which he comes to kindle in each one of us. . . The Heart of Christ is the Centre of the Christian mystery and key to the universe.'

Paul Leonard, S.J.
Dublin, 31st May 1983.

PREFACE

History sometimes highlights spiritual experiences which have no precedent. The roots may already be present in the person's past, but these experiences are unforgettable and become a permanent norm for as long as whoever lives these experiences is alive to conserve their identity. This is true also of the Church which will survive until the end of time and which will never lose its identity. Although an analogy with the Church may not be as apposite as it should, yet both in the Church and in Religious Orders, these experiences for the most part have evident repercussions only when foundational experiences are involved, e.g. in the early Church or at the time of our Founder. It is right therefore that these experiences be acknowledged as having the value of norms for the future.

However, in the recent history of the Church and of a Religious Order, there are certain experiences which, at least in analogy, acquire and conserve the value of an established norm. Without wanting to write a history of the devotion to the Sacred Heart of Jesus within the Society of Jesus, we can claim with some authority that this Society had in a period of its history an experience which it accepted to the full. Even though the devotion to the Heart of Jesus started only 200 years after the Society of Jesus was founded, it forms part and parcel of what the Society undertook from Christ. As such, the Society practises this devotion which it feels committed to spread. The fact that today this undertaking has become more difficult to carry out, and that the forms of worship may have to be redefined theologically and perhaps be lived and preached in accordance with current trends, does not in any way mean that the official and collective conscience of the Society has lost any conviction or that the devotion is any the less important an undertaking from God.

This brings us to a reality which is difficult to understand from a theological point of view, or indeed in the context of the history of spirituality. It is nevertheless worthy of further consideration that we are dealing with a Society that experienced something which does not date back as far as its origins, but nevertheless an experience that actually merges with the essence of the Society and cannot be reduced to a simple and trivial historical fact.

It is against this background that one should read these texts of the 28th Father General of the Society of Jesus, Father Pedro Arrupe. These texts are evidence of this fidelity to a celestial mission which his Society has accepted as an essential part of its *raison d'être*. They vouch for the passion with which the Society has maintained its identity throughout history, even when (in times like the present) the crisis of identity is knocking on the doors of religious orders. The inheritance of a devotion such as this could not be interpreted as a simple phenomenon to be dismissed as a simple outdated story. It is evident that this fidelity cannot be brought about by a reactionary form of conservatism. The transmission of such a legacy demands a creative fidelity (thereby giving a renewed vitality to the inheritance) and a reappraisal from the theological and pastoral points of view.

Father Arrupe has set his heart on this mission. The high degree of preparation which qualifies him for this is very obvious from his own personal life and indeed from the pastoral views he has expressed. The texts from this book stress how Father Arrupe interprets the *aggiornamento,* the updating of devotion to the Sacred Heart of Jesus.

If this form of worship is transmitted against a background of the immense task the Church has undertaken, for the new age and for always, to spread the Gospel in every place and culture, it will be more than obvious that the effort to transmit this living form of devotion to future generations inside and outside the Society, cannot be exhausted within the confines of this book. But it is another step in that duty of transmitting, and as such a sign of the fidelity to an unrenounceable experience of the Society, as well as a sign of an unyielding and fervent hope in the premise that from a saint in the past can be born a future full of promise.

Whatever Fr Arrupe contributes to this living reinterpretation of the devotion to the Sacred Heart must be gauged by the reader himself. I should just like to draw his attention to three points in order to avoid undervaluing Fr Arrupe's treatise.

Fr Arrupe makes use of the concept of *Urwort*[1] to deepen the understanding of the term Heart in this devotion. He is thus gearing all future theology related to this devotion towards this modern approach and towards the situation in which this modern science can contribute to a deeper understanding of religious language.

Fr Arrupe reminds us constantly of the prerequisites necessary for the full appreciation of the devotion to the Heart of Jesus. Consequently, he asks of the theology of this devotion an analysis of the subjective conditioning factors necessary to understand the devotion: in other words, we are advised not to miss the wood for the trees in this theology of faith and to follow in this branch of philosophy a trend which is perfectly compatible with modern theological thinking.

Finally, Fr Arrupe synthesizes the devotion to the Heart of Jesus in a context of the theology of love. It is in that sole love that he sees the inseparability of the love of God and the love of one's neighbour. This devotion can thus find its profound justification in the double mission which the Society undertook in its 32nd General Congregation — the struggle to preach the Gospel for the greater glory of God, and for human justice, without which man's total salvation would be impossible. Hence, the unity of love for God and love for one's neighbour are so inextricably bound up in the devotion to the Sacred Heart, that the devotion is sure to have a future within Fr Arrupe's Society and within the Church as a whole.

Karl Rahner S.J.
Innsbruck, 1st September 1982.

---

1   Cf: pp. 59, 87, 116, 123.

PART I

INSTRUCTIONS TO HIS FELLOW JESUITS

THE DECREE ON DEVOTION TO THE SACRED HEART OF JESUS

31st General Congregation of the Society

The fifteenth decreee of the thirty-first General Congregation (1965-66) on the Sacred Heart of Jesus was in response to numerous requests from various Jesuit Provinces throughout the world. When the matter was first discussed by the delegates, Father General himself recommended that the Congregation should respond to these requests. He and Fr J. Oñate drew up a Schema which was later presented to the appropriate Commission. This, in fact, was the final decree voted on in the Congregation and this was so because on the day when the votes were taken, Fr General Arrupe was absent from the meeting,preparing his closing address. The delegates, out of deference to him, waited his return so that he, too, might have the opportunity of exercising his right to vote on a decree so close to his heart. This same decree was confirmed by the 32nd General Congregation on December 11th, 1975, n.43.

T he Second Vatican Council has shed a brilliant new light upon the mystery of the Church, but this mystery is perceptible only to eyes directed in faith to the 'eternal love of the Incarnate Word'. For Christ, who 'thought with a human heart',[1] sacrificed himself in human love that he might win as his bride the Church which was born from his side as he slept on the cross.

---

1   Vat. II, *Gaudium et Spes*, N. 22.

The Church finds a splendid symbol for this love, at once human and divine, in the wounded heart of Christ, for the blood and water which flowed from it aptly represent the inauguration and growth of the Church[2] and solicit our response of love. Devotion to the Sacred Heart, as proposed by the Church, pays tribute to 'that love which God has shown us through Jesus, and is also the exercise of the love we have for God and for our fellowmen',[3] effecting that personal exchange of love which is the essence of Christian and religious life. This is why devotion to the Sacred Heart is regarded as an excellent and tested form of that dedication 'to Christ Jesus, king and centre of all hearts, which our age urgently needs, as Vatican II has insisted'.[4] This should be the concern of the Society above all, both among its own members and in its apostolic ministry, not only because of our long and venerable tradition but also because of the very recent recommendation of the Roman Pontiff.

For these reasons the General Congregation readily embraces the wishes of the Supreme Pontiff; it recalls the decrees of earlier Congregations concerning devotion to the heart of Christ[5] and urges all members of the Society to 'spread ever more widely a love for the Sacred Heart of Jesus and to show all men by word and example that the renewal of minds and morals, as well as the increased vitality and effectiveness of all religious institutes in the Church, which are called for by the Second Vatican Council, ought to draw their chief inspiration and vigour from this source.[6] In this way we shall more effectively make the love of Christ, which finds its symbol in the devotion to the Sacred Heart of Jesus, the centre of our own spiritual lives, proclaim with greater effect before all men the unfathomable riches of Christ, and foster the primacy of love in the Christian life.

It is no secret, however, that devotion to the Sacred Heart, at least in some places, is today less appealing to Jesuits and to the

---

2 Vat. II, *Lumen Gentium*, N. 3.
3 Pius XII, *Haurietis Aquas*, (AAS 48, 1956, 345).
4 Paul VI, *Investigabiles divitias*, (AAS 57, 1965, 300).
5 Decrees of the 23rd, 26th, 28th, 30th, General Congregations of the Society of Jesus (Col. decr. 223; 286; (90); (370).
6 Paul VI, *Diserti interpretes*, (Acta Romana XIV, 1965, 585).

faithful in general. The reason for this is, perhaps, to be found in outmoded devotional practices. Therefore our theologians, men experienced in spirituality and pastoral theology, and promoters of the apostolate of the Sacred Heart of Jesus are urgently asked to search out ways of presenting this devotion that are better suited to various regions and persons. For, while preserving the essential nature of the devotion, it would seem imperative to set aside unnecessary accretions and adapt it to contemporary needs, making it more intelligible to the men of our time and more attuned to their sensibilities.

The General Congregation also recommends that Father General encourage these studies. He will then be in a position to assist the whole Society to a better renewal of its religious and apostolic spirit.

THE SIGNIFICANCE OF THE HEART OF JESUS TO THE SOCIETY

Homily given at Valladolid, 1970

Fr Arrupe, for the first time after his appointment as General, visited Spain in 1970. In Valladolid he was particularly pleased to concelebrate Mass with a large group of Jesuits in the Sanctuary of the Great Promise, the Church of our former College of St Ambrose where it is said that the Sacred Heart conveyed special messages to Fr Bernardo Hoyos (14th May, 1733). This homily, as Fr Arrupe was to recall several years later, expresses his most deeply held convictions.

We bear this *munus suavissimum* in the carrying out of our apostolate of devotion to the Sacred Heart which is so fundamental to our spirituality, and which sometimes, as a result of a series of misinterpretations, has been neglected and ignored. So, I am truly glad today to be able to say that the Society of Jesus feels very united in this devotion to the Heart of Jesus; because it sees in this devotion what the various Popes have told us so often, that it encompasses the whole of Christian doctrine.

To be sure, the Society of Jesus has only one ideal, and that is to serve the Church, to serve 'the People of God', and to bring Christ to God's people. And we know that this Christ is discovered when we penetrate the secrets of his Sacred Heart, which is on the one hand a symbol of his love and on the other the living organ which pulsates with love, with Christ's love for all mankind.

Understanding the Whole Christ

Our understanding of Christ is the basis of all wisdom. And Christ, who is 'the Way, the Truth and the Life', can only be known through the very moving image which is imprinted on each page of the Gospel when it is read meditatively. As a personality he is sublime, immense and infinite; the gentle Christ who talks with the children; the Christ who thunders against the hypocrisies of the Pharisees; the Christ who, in Gethsemane, became absorbed in his heavenly Father; the Christ who commands the winds and calms the storm; the Christ who talks simply and who at the same time preaches doctrines which will never be fully understood by man because of their infinite profundity. And when we try to explain the authenticity of Christ, we come to see that there is one tremendous aspect of his nature, that he is, indeed, the Saviour of the World. And all the pages of the Gospel explain the process of salvation through this sublime and divine Person.

Christ is Saviour because he saved mankind, because he saved me: *Dilexit me et tradidit semetipsum pro me.* But if we ask ourselves whether that is the ultimate reason for the Gospel, and whether that is the ultimate love which is revealed through each page of the Gospel, we would have to say that the explanation goes much deeper than this; because the love for mankind, which Christ revealed, has its roots in the infinite love of the Blessed Trinity, in the love of the Word for the Father. That is to say, each line and letter of the Gospel is but an expression of the infinite love with which Christ wants to love and redeem mankind in order to give glory to his Eternal Father.

Moreover, were we to ask if that is the complete picture of Christ, our answer would again be that there is something deeper. For Christ gave himself up for us, died for us, but then rose from the dead for us. And Christ today is a living person. Where is he? In heaven, at the right hand of the Father, interceding for us. And he is also present in the Holy Sacrament, Christ in the Eucharist. Now, if we try and explain this interceding in heaven and this actual presence in the Most Holy Sacrament, we see that it is Christ's infinite love for mankind which explains why he wants to remain with us always.

Well then, the historic Christ, the risen and glorious Christ, the Eucharistic Christ, must surely summarize the whole of Christ's personality! Saint Augustine would not agree: 'If you want to love the whole Christ you have to open wide your heart; because Christ is the Head of a Body in Heaven, at the right hand of his Father, but he is also present throughout the world in each member of this same Body . . . in each one of us'. It is of the Mystical Christ, of the Mystical Body of Christ, of the whole Christ, that we are members.

Nor is that all, because we know that the only Person in Christ, who is the Word, is found at the depths of our own hearts. For this reason St Bernard asks the questions: 'Where is he who speaks to us in the depths of our hearts? How did he gain entrance? Did he come in through my eyes? Did he come in through my ears? Did he come in through my sense of touch?' And his answer is: 'No, because this is my most intimate sign. This, which is deepest in me, has been there from the beginning of my existence. It did not have to come in through any door. This divine Word in the depths of my soul, who talks to me, is also the Person of Christ, the whole Christ whose infinite love is symbolized in his Heart which is longing to manifest itself within me'.

Bring this Christ to the People of God

This is why we in the Society of Jesus have no other aim but to bring this whole Christ to the People of God at this historic time, which is so interesting yet so full of uncertainty, and in which a cultural evolution is taking place which appears to be giving birth to a new era, a new humanism of technology.

Now we Jesuits, together with all of you, are trying to discover how best to bring Christ to the people. For this reason, this moment of great historical interest is one which poses great difficulties, the solution to which can only be dictated by Christ himself: *Christus solutio omnium difficultatum*. Christ, whose essence is love symbolized by the heart, is the same gentle Christ of 2,000 years ago, at once powerful and weak, and who died on the Cross for us. He is the same one who is here present in the Holy Sacrament, and even more closely present in the depths of our souls. In him we shall find the solution to all our problems.

All of us, whether priests, religious or layfolk, all of us have to share responsibility and realize that it is not easy, since the philosophy that 'God is dead' is more widespread than we had suspected. Let us not content ourselves only with those ceremonies which have a consoling effect, rather let us remind ourselves that outside the Church a large proportion of God's people do not go to Church, either because it is physically impossible or out of ignorance or of malice. We must see ourselves as heralds of Jesus Christ; we must go out and contact those people, who in many cases even with much good will, find themselves alienated from the flock of Jesus Christ. This is the apostolic thrust; this is the desire to work for Christ; this is the desire to bring Christ to the people, and the people to Christ, in order that total triumph of Christ our Lord may soon become a reality.

Confidence in the Sacred Heart

To help us to fulfil our responsibilities as religious, we have that promise of the Sacred Heart which assures us of extraordinary graces, graces which we need today to combat atheism and to enable us to bring Christ into our secular world. For it is only Christ himself who can inspire us to undertake this work, as it is only he who can give us the hope and the strength to bring it to a successful conclusion. And that is why, today, the devotion to the Heart of Christ will prove to be of immense help when it is properly understood theologically. Indeed, each day that passes, it is becoming better understood and appreciated within the Church.

In an age when so many new sources of energy are being discovered; at a time when scientific research is held in the highest esteem — nuclear physics and atomic energy, which could transform our present day world — at such a period in human history we seem to be failing to realize that mere human discoveries, abilities and achievements are as nothing when compared with the superhuman power of the love of Christ, who gave his life so that he might bring life to all our world of men and women. We mere mortals, human beings as we are, can only discover and harness whatever sources of energy already exist in our world. Yet we believe that there exists a supernatural energy, not of this world, and that the source of this energy is Christ's infinite love. So, if we want to change our world for the better — socially, religiously, personally and on the level of the family — we have, here in the infinite love of Christ, the only energy that can make such a change. Saint Paul recognized this when he wrote: *Dilexit me et tradidit semetipsum pro me* (Gal. 2:20).

Since this is our faith, during this very moving concelebrated Mass, we are going to unite ourselves to that immense supernatural energy, the source of Christ's passion which is about to be renewed and offered on this altar. Let us pray that some of this superhuman energy, generated on this altar, may escape into our unbelieving world and bring the light of faith and the warmth of love to a sceptical and cold people. United to that generous Heart who knows and loves all who are in the world, we will offer his Sacrifice and ours with a like generosity of heart as we pray: 'Lord, hasten the day when every man will have his daily bread and make our world your own. May the power of your Mystical Body be extended more and more each day so that it may soon be possible to say truly that you are, in fact, the Head of all humanity'. This is why we will offer together this Holy Sacrifice with the utmost devotion, asking Christ Our Lord to grant these graces and petitions.

FACING A NEW SITUATION

An Open Letter to the Society of Jesus, 1972

*On 27 April, 1972, Father General Arrupe wrote a
letter to the entire Society, to announce officially that
on the 9 June, in the Church of the Gesù in Rome, he
would renew the Consecration of the Society to the
Heart of Jesus made by his predecessor, Fr Peter
Beckx, a century earlier. With this in mind he
examines the difficulties experienced by some Jesuits
with regard to devotion to the Heart of Jesus since the
Second Vatican Council.*

This is a theme very close to my heart, in spite of the fact that
today it is a difficult theme owing to the diversity of the subjective
attitudes toward this devotion prevalent among the members of
the Society. I shall limit myself to sharing with you a desire which I
feel very deeply as General: that is, to find a solution to the
ascetical, pastoral and apostolic problems which arise in the
devotion to the Sacred Heart today.

No one doubts that Ignatian spirituality is Christ-centred. Just
as is the case with our apostolate, it is totally based on the
knowledge of Jesus Christ the Redeemer, who has loved his Father
and the human race with a love that is human and divine, infinite
and personal, with a love that embraces each and every human
being. It is this love of Christ — which a centuries-old tradition, re-
inforced by the *Magisterium*, centres in his heart — that gives rise
to the apostolic response (in the Ignatian manner) of 'those who

wish to distinguish themselves in his service'. And it is these who come to that complete self-abandonment to the Cross (the *kenosis* of the *Vexillum Crucis*), which enables them to collaborate in the redemption of the world.

Two Opposing Attitudes

That Ignatian spirituality is Christ-centred is a fundamental point upon which we can easily agree. But when it comes to devotion to the Sacred Heart, there are two opposing attitudes which might be characterized as follows: there are those who consider this spirituality, which has been and continues to be called the 'devotion to or cult of the Sacred Heart of Jesus', so essential and so much a part of the Society that they consider it indispensable for every good Jesuit. The apostolate of the Sacred Heart, *munus suavissimum,* would be for such not only an essential element of all our pastoral activity but would be the very heart and inspiration of it. The Sacred Heart, symbol of the divine/human love of Christ, would be for them the most direct way of arriving at the knowledge and love of Jesus Christ.

On the other hand there are other Jesuits who feel a pronounced indifference to and even a sort of sub-conscious aversion from this type of devotion; they even go so far as to avoid all mention of it. In fact, they think that it consists only of a few old-fashioned and anachronistic devotional practices which are of no help at all. They feel also that the heart-symbol is equally valueless since, according to them, the word *heart* has become charged with sentimentality and an immutable allegorical meaning. This is further complicated by the fact that, at least in some cultures, the heart is not even used as a symbol of love except in a purely sentimental context.

The result of all this is that many people are confused about the whole matter. They are convinced of the value of the essential idea of faith in the Heart of Christ, but have no idea of how to present it to others in a manner acceptable and appropriate for our times. They prefer therefore to maintain a respectful silence and await some acceptable development.

These two attitudes would seem to be irrevocably and essentially opposed, but perhaps this is not so, at least in their basic premises. The first is based, as nobody can deny, on numerous official documents of the Church and on the traditions of the Society, on decrees of the General Congregations, on letters of the Fathers General, etc. A formation of this sort, beginning from the novitiate, and fostered by individual experiences, both spiritual and apostolic, clearly demonstrates the extent to which many Jesuits have found support from the practice of this devotion, and not a few recall the *ultra quam superaverint* in the extraordinary fruits of their apostolic activity as a faith-inspiring sign of its efficacy.

The second attitude finds its origins in a series of reasons, which will vary with each individual case. I am not, of course, referring to those deeper problems which are based on a Christological difficulty which can even go so far as to damage our very faith in Christ and our personal relationship with him, but rather to various other causes which contribute to the serious reservations of some among us. They feel, in effect, a general difficulty in accepting the methods of a spirituality which can, according to them, signify a limitation of personal freedom, or which might give the impression of something which is indiscriminately imposed from outside. Others fear to compromise themselves by a spirituality which they imagine to be too highly subjective and intimate. Yet others are put off by an excessive value placed on private revelations, which are sometimes presented as the sole source of devotion to the Heart of Christ and by the concept of consecration or dedication itself. And not a few instinctively reject the devotion because of its emotional content or because of the lack of artistic taste and the tawdriness of some of the statues, pictures and even writings connected with this devotion.

Toward a True Discernment

If these two attitudes are compared in an atmosphere of serenity and with true spiritual discernment as the goal, they are not so contrary as they might appear to be. When we analyse the significance of expressions such as, 'Deliver me from those special devotions; Jesus Christ, Redeemer, crucified and risen is enough for me', it is very clear that what is paramount in them is the fundamental nature of a true love of Christ who in the Paschal mystery has brought about our redemption and calls us to intimate union with him; it is precisely this unconditional love of the Person of Christ which has always been an essential element in the devotion to the Sacred Heart.

When those who take the second attitude suggest the rejection of practices that are unacceptable today, those of the first have no difficulty in recognizing that these are only accidental and of relative value. If the latter, in turn, insist that a love which is Christ-centred and personal is absolutely necessary for a vocation in the Society, the former accept it fully, realizing that one could over-emphasize the horizontal dimension if one loses sight of the indispensable vertical dimension.

One could also mention other points which, in a balanced discernment, lose their aggressiveness and even disappear. We should encourage this interchange of ideas which should have the following characteristics, typically Ignatian:—

● A broad openness which tries to understand the proposition and its proposer (Spir.Ex. n.22).

● Complete objectivity; recognizing real values and eliminating every type of unilateral exaggeration or emotional reaction (Spir. Ex. n.181).

● Full respect for the legitimate freedom of others, without wanting everyone to take the same approach, but allowing the Spirit to lead each according to his will (Spir. Ex. n.15).

A Decisive Argument
The objective value of true devotion to the Heart of Christ is shown both in daily life and in many documents of the Church and of our Society. It would be difficult to maintain, and even more difficult to prove scientifically, that its foundations are false or lack theological grounding, when one considers the profound nature of the message which it offers and the response which it requires.

Christ, the God-Man, and precisely because he is the incarnate Son of God, is in full possession of all truly human attributes. He is God and at the same time he is the most human of men. Christ is the realization of the full measure of love, because he is the expression of the gift God made to us of his Son, clothed in flesh, and because he is in himself a synthesis of the perfect love of the Father and of mankind.

It is this mystery of the divine/human love, symbolized in the Sacred Heart of Christ, that the traditional devotion to the Sacred Heart has tried to understand and tried to emphasize in a world that is day by day more in need of love and understanding and justice. In this relationship between the Word of God and the Heart of Jesus Christ pierced on the Cross, lies the whole humanity of the Son of God; and the dimming of the true theological sense of that humanity has been one of the reasons for the dethronement of his Heart as a symbol. To belittle the total humanity of Christ is equivalent to the creation of a theological abyss between the symbol and what is symbolised which the anthropomorphists and the pietists attempt to fill. To leave in the shadows the full humanity of Christ also implies the complete loss of the communitarian dimension, that is to say, the ecclesial dimension of Christ-centred spirituality. For the Church was born out of the Incarnation; more than that, she is a continual incarnation; the Church is the Mystical Body of God-made-man. So then, there is nothing less individualistic than a genuine love of Christ. Indeed, the very existence of reparation also proceeds from an authentic communitarian demand of the Mystical Body.

While trying to overcome the psychological problem that the external forms of this devotion can cause, the Jesuit must revitalize his devotion with the solid and virile Christ-centred spirituality of the *Exercises* which, with their integral Christ-centralism and their culmination in total commitment, prepare us to *feel* the love of the Heart of Christ as the unifying point of everything in the Gospels. The life of the Jesuit is completely unified by the response to the Eternal King and in that 'Take, Lord, and receive', of the Contemplation for obtaining love, which is the crowning point of the *Exercises*. Living this response and this offering is for each one of us, and for the Society as a whole, the true realization of the spirit of dedication to the Heart of Christ in its Ignatian sense.

It is from this intense 'living out' the spirit of the *Exercises* that there springs up an inescapable, apostolic urgency, a determination to live and to offer prayers and personal actions in union with the Heart of Christ, and in this way to live one's life intimately centred in Christ and in the Church. The Apostleship of Prayer has renewed and will continue to renew the priestly perspective of so many Christian lives, leading them to participate in the Eucharistic offering of Christ and in the consecration of the world to God.[1] This power of the Apostleship of Prayer, which has been of such help to God's people in the past, can also, if it is energetically renewed and adapted, offer new and greater service today, when we feel so strongly the need to create apostolic prayer groups with serious spiritual commitments.

Facing the Difficulty with Hope

It is a fact that, in diverse historical situations, the Providence of God has always provided for the Church the most appropriate spiritual tools. It is clear that for the Society of Jesus one such has been the devotion to the Sacred Heart. No one can deny the excellent fruits of it as evidenced in the Christo-centric spirituality and the apostolate of the Society. It is theologically true and confirmed by the tradition of the Society that the devotion to the Sacred Heart has been a tool of immense value and that this value can and ought to be applied to present-day circumstances.

On the other hand, it is equally true that we are faced with the fact that today many good Jesuits feel no special attraction to this form of prayer and, indeed, feel a definite aversion from it. And it is an Ignatian principle that no one may impose upon another a form of spirituality which does not help him to be a good Jesuit.[2] Historically, we are living in a time of criticizing, of questioning and even of rejecting traditional elements. This, although it is fraught with danger, has the good effect of making us delve deeply into the essence of things.

---

1 *Lumen Gentium,* n.34.
2 M.I. Fontes Narrativi IV — 855.

From all this we can conclude that the Society, precisely in order to remain faithful to her traditions, has the duty of studying the essence of the devotion to the Sacred Heart and of discovering the best way to use it and to present it to the present-day world. Simplistic solutions which either ignore the necessity for a living adaptation of the devotion and for the theological development of its essence and practice, or which reject it out of hand because it is personally unattractive, all these are quite unacceptable. To delve deeply into this spiritual, pastoral and apostolic problem will lead us, on the one hand, to discover a true solution which will be of great value not only to us ourselves but to those other religious and lay people who are quite confused and who await some sort of concrete help in the matter. On the other hand, it will dispose us to know more deeply him in whom are to be found all of the treasures of wisdom and knowledge. (Col. 2:3).

The profound study of the pierced side of Jesus on the Cross (Jn. 19:34) is a fruitful and timely theme for reflection. The Evangelist who had expressly emphasized the love of Christ in his passion and death (Jn. 13:1, 15, 13), seems to wish to call our attention to this love which is the keystone of the redemptive work, by showing us the open side of Jesus from which flows blood and water, a symbolic announcement of the gifts of the Holy Spirit to the Church.

A Personal Addendum

In my capacity as General I should like to add a personal word. I have been deeply aware of the obligation to treat this vital· aspect of our spirituality, not only because we are celebrating this centenary, but also because, apart from my personal conviction of the great value of the devotion to the Sacred Heart of Christ and its place as a source of energy (this for theological reasons as well as from personal experience) I feel that it can, in fact, be classified as a 'compendium of the Christian religion', as several Pontiffs have said, and as Paul VI put it, 'an excellent form of true piety . . . for our times'.

This brings me to recommend to everyone and especially our theologians and those who are specializing in spirituality and pastoral theology, that they study to discover the best manner of modern presentation so that in the future we may obtain the same results that were forthcoming in the past. I am convinced that in insisting on this I am acting in the best interests of the Society, and that to the extent that we more deeply penetrate the love of Christ, it will be that much easier for us to find the true means of describing it and expressing it. The promised *ultra quam speraverint* will apply to us as well.

In the Roman Church of the Gesù, where Fr Beckx first made the consecration of the Society to the Sacred Heart of Jesus, I intend to renew it on June 9th, using the very same formula.[3] I hope that, in each Province and in the manner considered most convenient, everyone unites himself with this act.

May the Father 'who has hidden these things from the wise and prudent and has revealed them to the little ones' (Matt. 11:25), grant us, you and me, the grace to know and feel, more and more profoundly, the inexhaustible riches hidden in the Heart of Christ. I consider this grace of the greatest importance at this moment in the history of the Church and the Society. *Petite et dabitur vobis.*

---

3 This formula was composed by a number of theologians; it was later replaced by the formula composed by Fr Arrupe himself which is reproduced in a later Section, p. 39.

THE CONSECRATION OF THE SOCIETY TO THE SACRED HEART OF JESUS AND THE VISION OF LA STORTA

Homily delivered in the Church of the Gesù in Rome 1972

On the 9th June 1972, the feast of the Sacred Heart of Jesus, Father Arrupe concelebrated Mass with 160 Jesuits in the Church of the Gesù in Rome, and in the presence of the congregation renewed the Society's consecration. In the homily he drew a parallel — and in this he was original — between the significance of the grace of La Storta and the consecration of the Society. True transcendence is to be united with Christ, 'to be placed with him'.

In renewing the consecration of the Society to the Sacred Heart which took place in this very Church of the Gesù a hundred years ago, I instinctively recall those times so difficult for the Society, when Father Peter Beckx performed the ceremony. He spoke thus: 'If we examine the state of the world, we begin to sense new ills and have good reason to fear others'. He added, 'Let us ask him (the Sacred Heart) for well-being, salvation, peace, and hope for these with unfaltering faith'.

As it was then, so is it now; the situation in the world and the Church is extremely delicate. We encounter today a new kind of world, a new breed of men, religious life in a state of evolution. Convinced that the solution for these difficulties and the ability to adapt our way of life to this new environment lie in him who is *solutio omnium difficultatum,* today we also wish to renew our consecration to the Heart of Christ.

In searching for a way of making our consecration relevant to the present and the immediate future, I have pondered on the 'espirito primigenio' of St Ignatius, evoking the Vision of La Storta.

The Vision of La Storta

One could ask: What has La Storta to do with the Consecration of the Society to the Sacred Heart? And really, on the surface there could scarcely be two events more distinct. In La Storta, a solitary and abandoned chapel in the suburbs of Rome, an impoverished pilgrim and two of his companions stopped to pray and in his innermost soul, in the intimacy of his spirit, the Trinity conferred on Ignatius a favour of the highest order, the summit of his mystic life until then, and the most decisive for the foundation of the Society of Jesus.

It was here in the Gesù that Father General Beckx, representing thousands of Jesuits, performed the ceremony of consecration, the echo of which spread to all the houses of the Society, scattered across the world. Upon closer scrutiny of the two events, one finds a clear relationship. The spiritual significance, the depth and richness of the experience at La Storta come across to Jesuits of today as a fountain of inspiration, as the best key to the interpretation, in the fullest Ignatian sense, of this consecration.

Ignatius had for many years petitioned Our Lady to 'place him with her Son'. This petition is now granted in a way more sublime than he had ever imagined. At La Storta, Ignatius received a profound understanding of his vocation: He is called to be the Companion of Jesus and the Holy Trinity accepts him as a servant of Jesus. It is the Eternal Father himself who 'imprints' his acceptance upon the soul of Ignatius and promises his special protection when he pronounces those words, which were preserved for us by Lainez: *Ego vobis Romae propitius ero* or the even stronger and more significant expression, which we can read in Nadal and Canisius, *Ego vobiscum ero.*

Later, turning to Jesus who appeared carrying his cross, the Eternal Father told him, pointing to Ignatius: 'I want you to take him as your servant', to which, looking towards Ignatius, Jesus replied: 'I want you to serve us'. This Trinitarian scene, described so briefly, denotes the giving of a mystic grace of the highest order — such that it could never be expressed adequately in human language. This was recognized by Ignatius and this is why there have been so many versions of this uniquely profound experience.

The Consecration: 'To be placed with the Son'

By analysing some of the details of the La Storta experience, we will be able to discern much of its significance. Ignatius' prayer is heard by no less than the Eternal Father. It is the Father who 'imprints' on Ignatius the unmistakable sense of divine protection. The *Ego vobiscum sum* — 'I will be with you' — is like an echo of the Biblical promises. It was thus that the God of Armies assured Gideon, *Ego ero tecum percutiens Madian.* Thus the God of Israel to the prophets, *Ne timeas quia ego tecum sum* (Is. 41; 10); *Ne timeas a facie eorum tecum ego sum* (Jer. 1; 8 and 19). Thus the Angel assured Mary, *Ave, gratia plena, Dominus tecum.* Thus Christ promised his Apostles, *Ecce ego vobiscum sum omnibus diebus usque ad consummationem saeculi* (Matt. 28:20) and Paul in Corinth, *Noli timere, ne taceas propter quod ego sum tecum* (Acts. 18:9,10).

Now Ignatius can feel secure. Who can overcome him if God is on his side? Ignatius' prayer 'To be placed with Jesus' is crucial. The phrase, although grammatically rather strained and rigid, expresses a radical desire of his — to obtain a more intimate closeness to Jesus than he already enjoyed; a reciprocated intimacy, similar to what St Teresa describes as 'spiritual wedlock' and Maria de la Encarnation as 'the gift of the Spirit of the Word Incarnate' (Lettre de 2.2.1649, Ecrits spirituels IV, 258-62). And, if Ignatius so ardently desired that grace, it was because he foresaw how necessary it would be for the realization of the apostolic ideal that was so much part of him.

The Eternal Father takes the initiative and passes on Ignatius' wishes to his Son Jesus: 'I want you to receive him into your service', and in turn Jesus, who always obeys the Father, replies, addressing Ignatius, 'I want you to serve us'. Not 'to serve me' but 'to serve us', thus receiving Ignatius into the service of the Holy Trinity. Ignatius' gift of self-offering is thus accepted by the Word Incarnate. A transformation takes place, more radical than that of the Cardoner. There, it seemed to him, that what happened was at the level of mind; here it goes much deeper; he *feels* accepted, introduced into the inner life of the Trinity, 'the intimate circle of the Trinity' (MI. SER. III, Vol. 1); and from there he is sent *ad extra* with Christ, in order to serve him on behalf of souls; a new kind of service which he would later define in the Formula of the Institute as, 'To serve the Church under the Roman Pontiff' or 'the defence and propagation of the Faith'.

The word 'serve' so characteristic of Ignatius acquires here its full meaning. It expresses the aim of the *Exercises;* it epitomizes the gift of the *Kingdom;* the meaning of the *Two Standards, The Three Degrees of Humility.* From now on to serve will mean whole-hearted consecration in the service of the Trinity, in companionship with Christ poor and suffering on the Cross. Ignatius understands the full meaning of his vocation and that of his companions and he feels not only called but accepted and inwardly transformed, as the apostles were. Such was his inner strrength that he feels himself capable of dying on the cross. 'I don't know what awaits us in Rome', he repeated, 'I don't know whether we will be crucified'. The grace of La Storta serves to light up the spiritual path of the Society and helps us to understand the meaning of our vocation in every historic situation: At the service of the Trinity with the poor Christ.

Sub Vexillo Crucis

Before the *munus suavissimum,* entrusted to the Society, of living and spreading devotion to the Sacred Heart, what meaning could there be in the consecration of the Society to the Sacred Heart a hundred years ago by Father Beckx? What meaning in the consecration which we wish to renew today other than to give ourselves wholly and unconditionally to the service of Jesus and the Trinity; to collaborate with Jesus poor — in order to give glory to the Father and help the world to find its salvation?

St Francis Borgia, St Peter Canisius, Bl. Claude La Colombière and so many other great Jesuits have thus understood the 'serve' under the standard of the Cross — *sub vexillo crucis* — taught by La Storta. Jesus appeared before Ignatius with the Cross on his shoulders. We see him today nailed to the Cross, his side pierced, his heart exposed — a sign of love — from which flow blood and water — a mystical symbol of his Church. The *Vexillum Crucis* thus acquires a new meaning, more personal, dynamic and profound; a permanent reminder that the mystery of the Incarnation and Redemption is rooted in the infinite and human love of Christ.

This constant awareness of what is most intimate in the personality of Christ, his love for the Father and for us is a new dimension added to the vision of La Storta, helping us to understand better its meaning, importance and relevance to us. That is to say, La Storta shows us the true Ignatian meaning of our consecration, and our consecration deepens our insight into the message of La Storta; so that knowing Jesus more intimately we have a better understanding of our mission, are more Ignatian and closer *socii Jesu*. What then is this consecration which is about to take place in a few minutes? 'Nothing other' says Leo XIII in *Annum Sacrum* (AAS XXXI, 649, 1899) 'than a total offering of ourselves, a radical committing of ourselves to Jesus Christ because what is given to the Heart of Christ is given to Christ'.

Here then is a commitment, a gift, an offering, a *suscipe*. It is an act of faith, an oblation to the Trinity and an absolute commitment to the Word Incarnate and to the Church, the Mystical Body, translated into special loyalty to the Vicar of Christ, referred to by Ignatius as the 'principle and foundation' of the Society. It is an act of hope because we know that for the strength to keep our promise we can count on the help of God; *Ego vobiscum ero. Si Deus pro nobis, quis contra nos?* We know from experience the many graces obtained through this devotion. It is an act of charity because we make our commitment as a sacrifice fully conscious of its consequences, well aware of the meaning of 'giving our lives for our friends' to follow the crucified Jesus.

In Today's World

The world needs men of faith, strong, disinterested, confident, ready to give their lives for others. This cannot come about without special graces; our vocation in the present world is too difficult. This is why we ask Mary to obtain from the Father, as she did for Ignatius, that special reciprocal intimacy which enables us not only to resist the world but also to bring it to Christ. A grace which will 'confirm' an inner transformation, a re-creation of all our faculties, an identification with Christ so complete that, to quote Nadal, 'We will understand through his understanding, love through his will, recall through his memory and that all our being, our existence and actions will not be in us, but in Christ'. (MN. S.J. Vol. 90, 122) — an inner transformation which moves us to a greater love of the Trinity, of Christ, of the Church and of souls, enabling us to reach the Ignatian standard of companionship with Christ Jesus. Finally, a grace which will change our hearts of stone into hearts of flesh, making us aware — fully aware — that God is always in and with us and that we may feel him — to use an Ignatian phrase, 'as a weight in our soul'.

Our consecration ends with the words of the *Suscipe* — the résumé and crowning of the *Exercises,* expressing our personal or special way of offering ourselves, of making the holocaust of ourselves concrete, *in odorem suavitatis.* And being accepted by the Lord, he guarantees us the graces necessary to put it into practice: *ad explendum, gratiam uberem largiaris.*

Once again we see the identification of the Spirit of the Consecration with that of the *Exercises* and the *Constitutions* and its most appropriate expression will be what implements the ideal of the true son of Ignatius and the companion of Jesus.

Let us end by thinking, like St Francis Borgia, of Christ our Lord on the Cross 'about the wound in his side, seeing it as a refuge, an oratory and a permanent abode'.

THE NEW FORMULA OF CONSECRATION OF THE SOCIETY TO THE HEART OF JESUS

Original Text, June 1972.

Father Arrrupe wished to change the formula of Consecration used by Father Beckx, because he considered that it belonged to another very different cultural age. He commissioned a group of theologians with the composition of a new text. Finally, on the advice of some Jesuits, he made use of the present form, which he himself had composed during a day of prayer at La Storta.

OEternal Father, while Ignatius prayed in the Chapel of La Storta, you wished as a special favour to accept the petition which for a long time he had made to you through the intercession of Our Lady: 'To be placed with your Son'.[1] You assured him also that you would be his support when you said to him 'I will be with you'.[2] You manifested your wish that Jesus, bearer of the Cross,[3] should admit him as his servant, which Jesus accepted, addressing himself to Ignatius with these unforgettable words: 'I want you to serve us'.[4]

We, the successors of that handful of men who were the first members of the 'Company of Jesus', repeat in our turn the same

---

1 'You wished to place him with your Son'. (Autobiography n. 96, FN. 1 496-7 cfr. MI, Const. I, p. 104).
2 'I will be with you'. (FN I 313; II 158).
3 Mon. Nadal V, 51.
4 'I wish you to serve us'. (FN II 133).

request 'to be placed with your Son' and to serve under the Standard of the Cross[5] on which Jesus is nailed by obedience, with side pierced and heart opened as the sign of his love of you, Father, and of all humanity.

We renew the consecration of the Society to the Heart of Jesus and we promise the fullest fidelity, asking for the grace to continue serving you and your Son with the same spirit and the same fervour of Ignatius, and his companions.

Through the intercession of the Virgin Mary who accepted Ignatius' petition and before the Cross from which Jesus hands over to us the treasures of his open Heart, we say today, through him and in him from the depths of our being:

'Take, O Lord, and receive my whole liberty, my memory, my understanding and my whole will, whatever I have and possess. Thou hast given me all these; To thee, O Lord, I restore them; all are thine; dispose of them in any way according to thy will. Give me thy love and thy grace, for that is enough for me.'[6]

On the Feast of the Sacred Heart, Church of Gesù, Rome. 9th June 1972.

---

5 'Under the standard of the Cross'. (Form. Inst. n. 1).
6 'Take, Lord. . . .' (Ex. 234).

REFLECTIONS ON THE APOSTLESHIP OF PRAYER

*Fr Arrupe's Address to an International Congress of
National Secretaries of the Apostleship of Prayer at
Rome, May 1974*

It is very important for us to understand the value possessed by the Apostleship of Prayer at the moment in which we are living; to be aware of the new favourable circumstances in which it is placed, and the effectiveness it can have in present circumstances; for today the world is arriving at a crossroads; not only that, but also at a time of creation of a new culture and a new humanity.

The history of mankind is the history of salvation; the philosophy of that history coincides with the theology of that history. It is the spirit of God — he who renews the face of the earth — who directs the history of humanity. Man makes his plans, but it is God who guides the world: 'A man's heart seeks out the way, but it is God who directs his steps' (Prov 16:9).

We are able to discern this hidden action of the Spirit by looking at the signs of the times. The world, social phenomena, the course of human history, all are as it were a book written by two authors: the Spirit of God and human liberty, united in collaboration and forming a community which is a true mystery: the mystery of Providence and infinite Wisdom on the one hand, and the mystery of human freedom on the other: 'We know that all creation is groaning in birth pains' (Rom 8:22).

The Apostleship of Prayer can and ought to be a great force for transforming the world. When I speak of the 'world', I do not mean it in a philosophical and general sense, but concretely and historically: as the generality of men and things that go to make up our present world. It is the world that the Vatican Council had in mind: '. . . the world of people, the entire human family together with the universe in which it lives. It is the theatre where the history of the human race is played out; the world marked by man's efforts, tragedies and victories. For it is the belief of Christians that this world was created and is maintained in existence by the Creator's love; it indeed fell into the slavery of sin, but, through the Cross and the Resurrection, Christ broke the power of the Evil One and liberated it in order that it might be transformed according to God's plan and so arrive at its accomplishment' (Gaudium et Spes n.2).

The transformation here mentioned is effected through the world being assumed into Christ 'so as to make a new creation beginning from this earth', which will attain to its fullness on the last day (cf. AA 5). The risen Christ is the beginning of this new creation — Primatum habens.

And this beginning is dynamically present in the Church — primitiae creationis novae — as a transforming force. This power works through the Word of the Gospel and the Sacraments, in the whole of the ecclesial Community, and it spreads to all creatures 'who await the manifestation of the glory of the Son of God' (Rom 8:19).

In the Church the Apostleship of Prayer is a privileged organ of this power. It 'canalizes' it, and makes it present and operative. It helps Christians to live and work with that power. It is thus a valuable means 'for bringing to perfection' our brothers and sisters in the Church which is the apostolic purpose of the Society.

Let us now look more closely at how the Apostleship of Prayer is an instrument for transformation of the world: let us look at the facts and the potentialities.

I should like to distinguish three levels which are closely linked: the individual Christian; the social dimension, the Church; the cosmic dimension, the world.

I. Transformation of the Christian's life

On the level of freedom, of free moral action: an essential for liberty is 'intention'. Let us give the word 'intention' its full force. Not intention as it sometimes is weakly understood, and conceived in an excessively exclusive voluntarist way, on the level of will, but rather let us consider it as belonging to the intellect above all, as in the usual scholastic tradition. Today, we might more readily speak of 'mentality', or of the 'dimension' of 'conscience. We could say that it is intention which gives form to the act. There can be several intentions in a single act. An intention may also be more or less specific.

The Christian's great intention is identification with the intention of God the Creator, as the Council said in the text already quoted: 'God himself wills to assume the whole world in Christ, so as to make a new creation of it' (AA 5); or as the *Exercises* put it in the *Foundation*. It is thus also identification — by the same token — with Christ's intention, as it is expressed in the *Kingdom* of the *Exercises*.

This intention was accepted by the Christian at the moment of baptism. But for Christian life to become more perfect there is need for this intention to transform ('inform') one's mentality and be able to become an 'actual' dimension of one's conscience.

The Apostleship helps to actualize or realize this intention by placing it in the forefront of one's consciousness; by bringing the great actual intentions of the Church before the mind.

This actualized and topical intention can transform man's life. By living in this new dimension the Christian will thus hear the appeal of God's will more intensely, and be readier to give a response.

Since this actualization of the intention is accomplished through conformity to the Church's great intentions, which are expressed by the Holy Father, the Christian will thus also live with the Church more intensely. So, we come to the social aspect, the Holy Father's great actual concerns at present, which ought to be integrated into the *Apostleship of Prayer*.

II. Transformation — conformation with and in the Church

It might seem tautological to speak of the ecclesial character of the

Apostleship of Prayer. Yet there are perhaps some community aspects in the life of the Church today to which the *Apostleship of Prayer* seems to remain, as I said, something of a stranger.

In the Church today there are many movements for community prayer; houses of prayer, prayer in family communities, in Communities of the Christian Life, rediscovery of common prayer in religious communities, and so many other forms. The Holy Spirit is at work in souls and in Christian groups.

We may here recall words which the Holy Father himself addressed to participants in a Congress of prayer groups: 'We rejoice with you at the renewal of spiritual life which is making itself known in the Church today under differing forms and in varying environments. Certain common features may be seen in this renewal . . . desire to give oneself totally to Christ, great readiness to respond to the calls of the Holy Spirit, more assiduous attention to Scripture, wide fraternal commitment, and a will to make a contribution to the Church's charitable works. In all this we may recognize the mysterious and discreet work of the Spirit, who is the soul of the Church . . .' (L'Osservatore Romano, Oct. 11, 1973, p. 2). We may also note that there are many Jesuits who take an active part in this movement.

Now, the *Apostleship of Prayer* is eminently ecclesial in its intentions, yet it has perhaps remained somewhat in the form in which it has so far been lived, rather limited to the 'individual dimension'.

I would wish that the *Apostleship of Prayer* might enter more completely into the multiform movement of solidarity in prayer which we are living in the Church today — without losing anything of its strength in the life of each Christian. May the *Apostleship of Prayer* live and express such solidarity in prayer not only through common intentions and by means of written communications, but may it also creatively develop group forms of prayer in common — in religious communities, in parishes, and so on, through the practice of prayer of intercession in the local communities. This prayer of intercession has perhaps been forgotten a little today, or at least it is not very much accepted, even though it is so natural and human.

This can be achieved also by entering into existing prayer groups, so as to make them more fruitful with the inspiration proper to the *Apostleship of Prayer*. Likewise, by co-operation with other active apostolic forces. Perhaps these groups are sometimes a little close, shut in on themselves. The importance of the Church's present intentions should be emphasized:

● by accepting the Holy Father's watchword for the Holy year, the reality of true reconciliation;

● by exploiting the possibilities which liturgical celebration gives us today for prayer of intercession;

● and in so many other ways that the Spirit will suggest to you. He himself, who gives to each and in each epoch *prout vult*.

III. Eucharistic transformation of the World

The *Apostleship of Prayer* has always had a Eucharistic character. It might be said that the Vatican Council made its own that spiritual attitude which is lived in the *Apostleship of Prayer,* when it said: 'All their works (the laity's), prayers, and apostolic endeavours, their ordinary married and family life, their daily labour, their mental and physical relaxation, if carried out in the Spirit, and even the hardships of life, if patiently borne — all of these become spiritual sacrifices acceptable to God through Jesus Christ (cf..I Pet. 2:5). During celebration of the Eucharist, these sacrifices are most lovingly offered to the Father, along with the Lord's Body. Thus, as worshippers whose every deed is holy, the laity consecrate the world itself to God' *(Lumen Gentium, n.34)*.

This consecration of the world is a transformation and a sanctification. The Council mentions this transformation and this sanctification when speaking to religious and laity:

'. . . By their state in life, religious give splendid and striking testimony that the world cannot be transfigured and offered to God without the spirit of the Beatitudes. But the laity by their very vocation . . . are called by God so that by exercising their proper function and being led by the spirit of the gospel they may work for sanctification of the world from within, in the manner of leaven' *(Lumen Gentium n.31).*

Men have been enabled by the paschal mystery to collaborate in the transformation of the human and natural world, which transformation is celebrated and mysteriously made present in the Eucharist, the 'Sacrament of the world'. For it makes all men free so that, putting aside love of self and bringing all earthly resources into the service of human life, they may devote themselves to that future when humanity itself will become an offering acceptable to God.

'The Lord left behind a pledge of this hope and strength for life's journey in that sacrament where *natural elements* refined by man are *changed* into his glorified Body and Blood, providing a meal of brotherly solidarity and a *foretaste* of the heavenly banquet' *(Gaudium et Spes, n.38).*

There is the power and dynamism of the *Apostleship of Prayer* in the world of the future, as the organ and instrument of that Eucharistic and ecclesial spirituality which lives from this great intention of the Church: 'Thus the Church prays and labours at the same time, in order that the fullness of the whole world may pass into the People of God, the Body of the Lord, the Temple of the Holy Spirit, and that in Christ, Head of all, all honour and glory may be rendered to the Creator and Father of the Universe' *(Lumen Gentium 17).*

Practical conclusions
What the Apostleship of Prayer could do:
How can the *Apostleship of Prayer* give practical aid to the modern world?

By teaching to pray: There is a real thirst for prayer, for contact with God, experience of God, dialogue with God. The 'Teach us how to pray' of Luke 11:1 is of vital relevance today. To teach how to pray is one of the prime apostolates of our day; it means collaborating with the Spirit and laying the basis for every other spiritual activity, both interior and apostolic. Without prayer there can be no *Apostleship of Prayer;* this is why the first apostolate of the Apostleship is to *teach how to pray.* And to pray in the twofold dimension which is of the individual and of the community. These are two aspects, two forms of prayer which complement each other and stimulate each other.

By showing the meaning and reality of the apostolate today. To expose the reality of the world and its dramatic character, and show how urgent it is for the world to arrive at a solution, which cannot but come from God, from God who is at work and is moving men to act according to his Spirit. When understanding is gained of the urgency of the apostolate and the difficulties it has to face, and when we consider the apostolate in all its breadth, it is much easier for prayer to arise spontaneously.

The Apostleship of Prayer as service to humanity. One of the groups has mentioned this idea: of giving the *Apostleship of Prayer* the sense of service to mankind; that is to say, to orient the Apostleship's prayer and spirituality in the direction of moving souls to the service of their neighbours in the whole vast range of services that the Church lays before us today as being proper for Christians.

This does not mean that we should go and transform the *Apostleship of Prayer* into a group of activists; neither should we reduce ourselves to a group which prays but has no awareness of its responsibilities and the necessity to co-operate effectively in finding solutions for the problems of the world about us. Today more than ever the world is sensitive to those words of the Apostle James: 'What benefit is it, my brethren, if a man say, I have faith, but have not works? . . . Faith, if it has no works, is really dead' (Jas 2:14-17).

It is necessary, therefore, to combine prayer with the service of action. This is a very Ignatian idea, and it is also dear to the present Pope, Paul VI (cf. *Octogesima Adveniens*, n. 48-49). It ought to be carefully meditated and considered with a view to integrating the service which the *Apostleship of Prayer* already gives through prayer with other kinds of service, of a social, charitable order, etc.

To teach in a modern manner what it means to be a *contemplativus in actione*, 'finding God in all things', *contemplata tradere*, expressions which denote a similar reality, even though there are shades· of difference in the ways of considering the spiritual life. In the spiritual man everything ought to tend towards the unity of a life oriented *ad maiorem Dei gloriam.*

Make much use of the liturgy — not only Holy Mass, which is always the centre of the entire liturgy, but also the liturgies of the word or the paraliturgies, adapting them in such a way as to lead the world of today to pray through the apostolate for the evangelization of men.

Cultivate a domain which has so far been neglected of praying together with separated brethren, and even with people of other religions, such as Islam, and with others that believe in the true God. This is an immense though sensitive field, and the *Apostleship of Prayer* can carry out valuable activity in it. It is certain that the Church's unity is the work of the Holy Spirit, and it is a mystery for the world of today how to gain that unity; yet it is no less certain that prayer for union and prayer, *uno ore et uno corde,* will be one of the most efficacious ways of arriving at complete union in the faith. Everything we can do in this regard will constitute excellent collaboration for that 'union of Christians' which the Church and the Holy Father have so much at heart.

What the Society of Jesus ought to do

Be convinced that the *Apostleship of Prayer* today retains its essential value, even though it has to be adapted to the modern world in its exterior manifestations and applications. We should even say that it is precisely in this age that it has its greatest value; hence we should make a serious and effective effort to make use of it to the full. For this reason it is for us (you and especially me) to try to present it to the Society in the most favourable way, demonstrating its relevance for our times.

Pray for the Apostleship of Prayer. In present conditions it will be very proper to pray to the Lord for the *Apostleship of Prayer* itself, so that he may enlighten us and help us to find solutions to the basic problems at present facing our organization. And let us be assured that if ever the Sacred Heart ought not fail to accomplish his promise to bless us 'beyond our hopes' and aid us, then it is very much the case today. It is for us to have much hope, *dilatando spatia caritatis et spei.*

Look for more collaborators. If the *Apostleship of Prayer* wishes to carry through a work as the efficacious result of its adaptation to the modern world, it needs more collaborators outside, but above all inside the Society. The difficulty of finding young people who will enthusiastically and competently help may be largely explained by the development going on in all sectors of the apostolate in the Church and in the Society of Jesus.

More concretely, in an apostolate like yours the difficulty is increased by the fact that numerous and varied problems are met with, of a theological, spiritual, psychological, pastoral order, etc. The *Apostleship of Prayer* is related to Christology, with the forms of spirituality, with the psychological significance of symbols, with ways of shaping pastoral action, and everything that that entails of diversity in devotions and exterior practices, which have marked the *Apostleship of Prayer* up to the present.

This is why I think that in order not to fall into a vicious circle — that is, not renewing ourselves because we have no young people and having no young people because we are not renewing ourselves — we ought to try to provide the *Apostleship of Prayer* with an inflow of youth, and at the same time make sure that traditional methods shall be open enough for them to be capable of being renewed and adapted.

We have to avoid two extremes: to expect young people to adapt to methods and a mentality they regard as old-fashioned, and to oblige present directors to abstract from an experience and tradition and even a doctrine which retains many solid and essential features, even though some of its elements have been superseded.

In order, then, to obtain real, spontaneous, and lasting collaboration from our own, it is necessary for us to be able to present this apostolate as something having great value for today; this is not a result to be obtained from arguments imposed from outside, but from conviction arising from inner experience and reasons and necessary openness to well-founded experimentation, subjected to periodic re-evaluation.

Reference has been made on many occasions to lack of collaboration on the part of Superiors of the Society. I think our effort at persuasion ought to begin with some of them. When they establish the priorities for their Provinces in all sincerity and with a sense of their responsibilities, perhaps they consider the *Apostleship of Prayer* as something that was valuable once but has lost its relevance for our day. We will not however, gain anything by throwing our faults up in each other's faces! We ought to make sincere efforts to engage in sincere dialogue so that all — superiors, those in charge of the *Apostleship of Prayer,* the young and not so young — may together rediscover those values that have to be rediscovered and give the *Apostleship of Prayer* an image and a reality which shall express all its present value and convince everybody of its importance.

That is the initial work we have to do, if we wish to see the *Apostleship of Prayer* bloom again and be renewed in the circumstances of our time. So, set to work as soon as you get back to your Provinces. We will do our part here.

Persevere in studying and adapting the way of presenting the devotion to the Heart of Jesus. This will be another great service which the *Apostleship of Prayer* can do for the Christian world today.

There is need not only for theological investigation, such as is necessary for gaining ever deeper knowledge of the 'riches of the wisdom of the knowledge of God' (Rom 11:3), but also for pastoral examination of how doctrine is expounded and devotion practised.

We cannot be blind to the difficulties which the latter presents today. It is a quite difficult point in catechetical pedagogy, and solving it calls for analysis of the various aspects of the problem: theological, psychological, affective, aesthetic, etc. These ought to be considered in a practical and up-to-date way. Clearly this also calls for openness, comprehension, prudence, and patience; this supposes that we know how to put ourselves in others' mentalities, and understand them without condemning them *a priori,* even though it may be sometimes very difficult for us to admit certain positions, expressions, or manifestations.

Conclusion: The Devotion to the Heart of Jesus

We ought to thank God for the gift he made of this devotion to the Society. It is our treasure. This devotion is characteristic of the

Apostleship of Prayer. It 'personalizes' this transforming force, makes it something personal.

The glorious Christ — he who showed himself to Thomas the Apostle and let him see the wounds inflicted by our sins, he who showed himself to St Ignatius at La Storta, bearing the Cross upon which he redeemed us — is he who has shown us his Heart transfixed on the Cross, a furnace of love.

This loving attention to Christ glorified, wounded by love, *agnus tamquam occisus,* reveals the sacrificial nature of this life of prayer and action for transformation of the world to which members of the *Apostleship of Prayer* commit themselves.

Sacrifice means suffering, which means total forgetfulness of oneself, which means dying to oneself. Sacrifice does not only mean patiently bearing with the adversities of life. The Christian spirit of sacrifice is a supremely active attitude, it is a gift of oneself — *et omnia sua* — in love, with generosity having divine dimensions; it is a bond of love in which man cries out: 'Lord, enclose me in the depth of your Heart. And, when you have me there, burn me, purify me, set me afire, raise me up to perfect satisfaction of your pleasure, unto the most complete annihilation of myself'.

A PRAYER TO JESUS CHRIST, OUR MODEL

Concluding his Address on 'Our Way of Proceeding'

*The Address of Fr Arrupe on the manner of life of the
Jesuit today, given during a Seminar held in Rome in
1979 is well known. We reproduce here the
conclusion of that Address. It not only illustrates his
very personal style of speaking but also the
importance he places in the Heart of Christ for every
Jesuit.*

Lord, meditating on 'our way of proceeding', I have discovered
that the ideal of our way of acting is your way of acting. For this
reason I fix my eyes on you; the eyes of faith see your face as you
appear in the gospel. I am one of those about whom St Peter says:
'You did not see him, yet you love him; and still without seeing
him, you are already filled with a joy so glorious that it cannot be
described, because you believe'. *Heb 12:2; 1 Pet 1:8.*

Lord, you yourself have told us: 'I have given you an example'
to follow. I want to follow you in that way so that I can say to
others: 'Be imitators of me as I am of Christ'. Although I am not
able to mean it as literally as St John, I should like to be able to
proclaim, at least through the faith and wisdom that you give me,
'what I have heard, what I have seen with my eyes, what I have
contemplated and touched with my hands concerning the Word

of Life. The Life manifested itself, and I have seen it and give witness'; although not with bodily eyes, certainly through the eyes of faith. *Jn. 13:15; 1 Cor. 11:1; 1 Jn. 1:3; (cfr. Jn. 20:25, 27); Lk. 24:39; Jn. 15:27.*

Above all, give me that *sensus Christi,* about which St Paul speaks: that I may feel with your feelings, with the sentiments of your heart, which basically are love for your Father and love for mankind. No one has shown more charity than you, giving your life for your friends with that *kenosis* of which St Paul speaks. But I should like to imitate you not only in your feelings, but also in everyday life, acting, as far as possible, as you did. *1 Cor. 2:16; Jn. 14:31; Jn. 13:1; Jn. 15:13; Phil. 2:7.*

Teach me your way of treating with disciples, with sinners, with children, with Pharisees, with Pilates and Herods; also with John the Baptists — before his birth and afterwards at the Jordan. Teach me how you deal with your disciples, especially the most intimate: with Peter, with John, with the traitor Judas. . . How delicately you treat them on Lake Tiberias, even preparing breakfast for them! How you wash their feet! *Lk. 17:16; Lk. 1:41-45; Matt. 3:17; Jn. 19:26-27; Jn. 13:26; Lk. 22:48; Jn. 21:9; Jn. 13:1-20.*

May I learn from you and from your ways, as St Ignatius did: how to eat and drink; how to attend banquets; how to act when hungry or thirsty, when tired from the ministry, when in need of rest or sleep. *Mk. 2:16; Jn. 4:8, 31-33; Jn. 2:1; Mt. 4:2; Jn. 4:7.*

Teach me how to be compassoionate to the suffering, to the poor, the blind, the lame, and the lepers; show me how you revealed your deepest emotions, as when you shed tears, or when you felt sorrow and anguish to the point of sweating blood and needed an angel to console you. Above all, I want to learn how you supported the extreme pain of the Cross, including the abandonment by your Father. *Mk. 9:36; 14:14; 15:32; Lk. 7:13; 19:41; Mt. 26:37-39; Mt. 27:46.*

Your humanity flows out from the Gospel, which shows you as noble, amiable, exemplary and sublime, with a perfect harmony between your life and your doctrine. Even your enemies said: 'Master, we know that you are truthful, that you teach the way of God in truth and care not for any man, for you regard not the person of men'. The Gospel shows your virile manner, hard on yourself in privations and wearying work, but for others full of kindness, with a consuming longing to serve. *Mt. 22:16; Mt. 8:20; Mt. 20:28; Cf. Phil. 2:7.*

It is true that you were hard on those in bad faith, but your goodness drew the multitudes; the sick and infirm felt instinctively that you would have pity on them; you so electrified the crowds that they forgot to eat; with a knowledge of everyday life you could offer parables that everyone understood, parables both beautiful and vigorous. Your friendship was for everyone, but you manifested a special love for some, like John, and a special friendship for some, like Lazarus, Martha and Mary. Show me how you expressed joy at festive gatherings; for example at Cana. *Mt. 9:36; 14:14; Mk. 3:20; Jn. 15:15; Jn. 13:23; 19:26; Jn. 11:36; Jn. 2:1.*

You were in constant contact with your Father in prayer and your formal prayer, often lasting all night, was certainly a source of the luminous transcendence noticed by your contemporaries. Your presence instilled respect, consternation, trembling, admiration, and sometimes even profound fear in various types and classes of people. *Mt. 26:36-41.*

Teach me your way of looking at people: as you glanced at Peter after his denial, as you penetrated the heart of the rich young man and the hearts of your disciples. *Lk. 22:61; Mk. 10:21-23; 3:34; 5:31-32.*

I should like to meet you as you really are, since your image changes those with whom you come into contact. Remember John the Baptist's first meeting with you? And the centurion's feeling of unworthiness? And the amazement of all those who saw miracles and other wonders? How you impressed your disciples, the rabble in the Garden of Olives, Pilate and his wife and the centurion at the foot of the cross. *Mt. 3:14; Mt. 8:8; Mt. 8:27; 9:33; Mk. 5:15; 7:37.*

The same Peter who was vividly impressed by the miraculous catch of fish also felt profoundly the tremendous distance between himself, a sinner, and you. He and the other Apostles were overcome with fear. *Mk. 1:27; Mt. 13:54.*

I should like to hear and be impressed by your manner of speaking; listening, for example, to your discourse in the synagogue at Caphernaum or the Sermon on the Mount where your audience felt you 'taught as one who has authority' and not as the Scribes. *Lk. 4:36; 5:26; Mk. 1:22.*

In the words of grace that came from your mouth the authority of the Spirit of God was evident. No one doubted that the superhuman majesty came from a close bond between Jesus and God. We have to learn from you the secret of such a close bond of union with God: in the more trivial, everyday actions, with that total dedication to loving the Father and all humanity, the perfect *kenosis* at the service of others, aware of the delicate humanity that makes us feel close to you and of that divine majesty that makes us feel so distant from such grandeur. *Lk. 4:22, 32.*

Give me that grace, that *sensus Christi,* your very heartbeat, that I may live all my life, interiorly and exteriorly, proceeding and discerning with your spirit, exactly as you did during your mortal life.

Teach us your way so that it becomes our way today, so that we may come closer to the great ideal of St Ignatius: to be companions of Jesus, collaborators in the work of redemption, each one of us an *alter Christus.*

I beg Mary, your most holy Mother who contributed so much to your formation and way of acting, to help me and all sons of the Society to become her sons, just like you, born of her and living with her all the days of your life.

PART 2

THE THEOLOGY OF THE HEART OF CHRIST

THE HEART OF CHRIST CENTRE OF THE CHRISTIAN MYSTERY AND KEY TO THE UNIVERSE

An Article published in 1981

This Article, written in January 1980, was published in English in the United States of America on the occasion of the first centenary of the Missionaries of the Sacred Heart. It is probably the most complete synthesis of the theological and existential thought of Fr Arrupe on the Sacred Heart.

The word 'heart', both in everyday language and in biblical terminology is one of those words which Karl Rahner has called an *Urwort*, that is a root-word, a parent-word which generates other words. Such words are packed with meaning and are very difficult to define, and for that reason are also highly evocative. Just as a small sea shell conjures up the roar and fury of the sea, such words stir up a rich variety of ideas and sentiments. The word 'mother' is another example. Who can say all that this word evokes? Or who can reduce it to a definition? To any definition of this word one can say 'yes, all that, but more', because no one can reach the very depth of its meaning, and even less can communicate it to others. The value of these words is precisely that we can understand each other's meaning when we refer to deep and complex realities. The psychology of language has in such words a subject for absorbing research.

But the very richness and depth of these words is, in part, their weakness. They are used so much in human communication that they become victims of abuse and end up cheapened and corrupted; or else they are watered-down so that they lose their flavour; or again, they are inflated and adapted to the fleeting fancy of the current vogue, then discarded abruptly. Fortunately nature always wins, and these words come to life again and bloom, their profound meaning and values intact.

'Heart of Jesus' is an expression that has suffered such vicissitudes. Marked with the symbolism and with the literary style and imagery of an era — which is necessarily fleeting — it seemed that it would remain buried beneath the wave of renewal. Not for long. 'Heart of Christ' is a phrase of unusual aptness and so rooted in biblical meaning that it is irreplaceable. It was sufficient to free it of superficial connotations for the original, rich and mysterious meaning to be restored. Heart of Jesus: all the love of Christ, God and man, sent by the Father, through the Spirit, who offers himself in redemption for all and with each of us establishes a personal relationship.

'. . . the inner mystery of man, in biblical and non-biblical language is expressed by the word "heart". Christ, the Redeemer of the world, is the one who penetrated in a unique unrepeatable way the mystery of man and entered his "heart"' (Redemptor Hominis, 8). 'In him human nature, by the very fact that it was assumed, not absorbed, has been raised in us also to a dignity beyond compare. By his incarnation, the Son of God has in a certain way united himself with each man. He worked with human hands, he thought with a human mind. He acted with a human will, and with a human heart he loved' (Gaudium et Spes, 22).

The Love of the Heart of Christ — Key to the Understanding of the History of Salvation

This gift which the Father has given us in the person of Christ is our salvation, the salvation of all men. Christ in his incarnation intervenes in the established relationship of man with God and completely transforms it. The great power which effects this revolution, the great novelty of the new Covenant is the love of his heart, and the love which he comes to kindle in each one of us. He has sealed this new Covenant with the sacrifice of reconciliation offered once and renewed in each Eucharistic celebration, a sacrifice completely acceptable and pleasing to the Father and gloriously sublimated in his resurrection.

The pristine catechesis and the Gospels derived from it are the story of this love. The four Gospels show us this love in action. This is especially true of the last chapters of St John's Gospel and of his letters — very particularly his first letter — where the theme of love becomes an exhortation, pointing us directly to the feelings and sentiments of the Heart of Christ, urging us to reciprocate his love.

Paul, for his part, spreads the 'Good News' throughout the whole world to all men, the news of our new condition, that we are a 'new creature'. The Old Law has been abrogated by God's love. In this way the fourth Gospel and the *corpus paulinum* marvellously complement and shed light on each other.

If the Old Testament is in essence the history of human tension in the presence of God the Creator, and can be summed up in the counterposition: 'heart of stone'/'new heart', the New Testament is summed up in the new relationship of love: *Cor Christi/cor hominis*, (Heart of Christ/heart of man). Thus, a term which is so typical in Semitic languages is raised in the New Testament message to a much higher level of meaning: the sentiments and acts of the Son of God and of each person in their reciprocal relationship.

Christ, defined by his Heart

It is impossible to find in the New Testament a word which more readily and accurately, more profoundly and with more human warmth, could come close to a definition of the person of Christ than his 'Heart'. Much of what John thinks and says of Christ is contained in the word *logos*, but there are many passages that do not fit that concept and also much of what the synoptics say is not contained in it; apart, of course, from the human characteristics which here and there bear out the rich personality of Christ. The word *logos* has a mental resonance that does not immediately 'describe' Christ. Rarely, on the other hand, do the Gospels reveal some interior characteristic of Christ that we cannot epitomize in his heart. Furthermore, the external signs, his parables and discourses, his whole life as presented in the Gospels — even considered as *Kerygma* — are not totally understood or understandable in all their profound meaning unless they are read from the angle of his heart. Read in this light, on the other hand, Jesus is seen whole and undivided in each moment of his life. All that he says and does in any instance gives us the measure of his inner being, of his infinite divine-human coherence: a person completely dedicated to the Mission received from the Father. And it is precisely these inner depths of Christ's life and being that we must try to discover through his words and deeds.

Consequently, it is not old-fashioned piety which makes us refer to the heart of Christ in order to sum up in one word all the values which we find in his person. There is no other expression more apt to convey 'the breadth and the length, the height and the depth of the love of Christ, which is beyond all knowledge' (Eph. 3:18), neither the *logos* of John, nor Wisdom, nor Son of Man, nor Messiah; not even the definitions which Jesus applied metaphorically to himself: Way, Truth, Life, Light, Good Shepherd, Bread, etc. Jesus himself, when he wanted to describe himself and his deepest sentiments, put aside all metaphors and used simple everyday language: 'Learn from me, for I am gentle and humble of heart' (Matt. 11:29).

Christ values the heart of each man

Christ judges each man by his heart. It is true to say that in the teaching of the prophets interior dispositions are already given considerable relevance; Jeremiah (4:1-4 and passim) and especially Ezekiel, and also that marvel, the language of the convert in Psalm 51, the *Miserere*. John the Baptist centres his preaching on the same theme and with the same stress as the prophets. Jesus also will do so but if love was previously implied in the sorrow of contrition ('crushing' of the heart), in the preaching of Jesus it is the other way round: it is remorse that is implied in love.

For Christ a man's coherence and integrity is of the essence. If there is one thing that really drives Jesus to holy indignation it is pharisaic insincerity, duplicity of heart, palming off the appearance of righteousness for love. Christ insists again and again that the goodness or badness of man is in his heart. The exaltation of man's inner being stresses a line along which the prophets had hardly advanced at all, namely, that it depends on man's inner self whether he is able to be incorporated into God's Kingdom. The Old Testament image of the Kingdom is now definitively replaced.

It is in the heart of man that, once the divine filiation is restored, the union between man and God is accomplished. The Kingdom, before its eschatological completion, is nothing else but the *ekklesia*, the community of those who through faith have received this interior transformation (Cf. 1 Cor. 1:2) and in brotherly union are on their way to their Father's house.

The central point in the relationship *Heart of Christ/heart of man* is love. More than faith, more than any other sentiment, it is love which transcendentally describes man and it is also love which comes closest to a definition of God. 'God is love'. Christ corresponds to the Father's infinite love with absolute loving obedience, and at the same time he loves man 'to the end' (Jn. 13:1). Christ's heart is the smelting vessel of his love for the Father as Word and as man, and also of his love for mankind. In the heart of man redeemed by Christ this love must find a proportionate response. This precisely is Paul's claim: 'He loved me and sacrificed himself for my sake' (Gal. 2:20). In the one divine person of Christ the two natures establish an encounter of love.

Christ: a New Concept of Love

The love of Yahweh in the Old Testament
From the beginning God took the initiative in the dialogue of love with man. But one cannot say that man completely understood or corresponded to the divine initiative. Biblical man 'knew' God, and for a Semite to know something is to have a certain experience of it, and in some way to love it. In the earlier period, the idea of God as Creator is paramount; God mysterious and distant who chooses his friends and confidants among men — the prophets and patriarchs. They are the witnesses of the drama of Yahweh's love and wrath. The people respond with adoration and obedience. Many of the Psalms both before and after the exile show that not only the people as a group or their leaders, but each individual and in particular each 'poor' one, each 'little' one, each 'just' one is loved by God.

But there are many questions still left unanswered. In what way is Yahweh's love interpreted? How does one respond to it? What is the relationship between the love of Yahweh and the love of one's neighbour? Yahweh is accepted as the one God, the Creator, the protector, the one who mysteriously rewards the righteous. His love is made tangible in his offer of the Covenant by which he weds himself to his chosen people. Israel's response can be nothing else but submission and fidelity, obedience to the law. This would be the meaning of the first precept of the decalogue: Love God 'with all your heart, with all your soul, with all your strength' (Dt. 6:5).

Even the Song of Songs, after all, is just a poetic exaltation of the alternate searching for and possessing of Yahweh and his people. Parallel to the prophetic line which presents the Covenant as a relationship of love, there is the legal line, which eventually predominates and increasingly insists on interpreting the Covenant in terms of accepting the law and obeying it: a law that becomes fragmented in countless precepts; an oppressive law which almost smothers love. Love of Yahweh turns into fear of Yahweh. The centre of gravity, so to speak, moves from the 'cordial' to the 'servile'. This fact provokes Christ's bitter reproaches against the Pharisees.

And perhaps it could not have been otherwise, since the revelation of the Trinity was yet to come. Love could not be perfect as long as men did not know God as Father, and were unaware of their kinship with the Son, and had not received the Spirit. And how could they have anticipated Yahweh's personal intervention in the history of his people by becoming one of them? Their idea of the Messiah was clouded by these obscruities. They expected a regal Messiah a priestly Messiah and, above all, a deliverer. The Messiah's relationship to God was still ill-defined and there was hardly an inkling of what his relationship to mankind would be. The veil which hid the mystery of the Trinity during the time of the Promise also concealed the fullness of God's love. The plurality of Persons was vague, barely a metaphoric intuition and therefore the One Sent could hardly be identified with one of these Persons. Furthermore the notion that the Chosen One should suffer and die was a scandal to the Jews. One can say that they were not ready for such love, for such overwhelming love. Christ, defined by his heart, surpasses all the expectations of the Old Testament and is established as the key to the whole history of salvation.

The Love of Neighbour in the Old Testament

The Old Testament also enjoins love of one's neighbour, but with obscure restrictions. True, the book of Leviticus completes the commandment about loving God with 'a second commandment': 'You must love your neighbour as yourself' (Lv. 19:18) and 'you must love the stranger as yourself' (Lv. 19:34) but 'neighbour' is practically the same as 'brother' that is to say, those who belong to the predestined race. Especially after the Exile, brotherhood has well recognized limits: the stranger who must be loved is a stranger (foreigner) passing by chance, or a resident: 'for you were strangers in the land of Egypt' (Dt. 10:18); but it excludes the gentiles, who, by definition, are enemies of God and consequently enemies of his people. The question 'who is my neighbour?' does not have a clear-cut answer, even for a well-intentioned Israelite. The less well-intentioned can give all sorts of wrong answers. Our Lord gives his own clear reply to this question in the parable of the Good Samaritan (Lk. 10:25-37).

The worst kind of hatred is hatred for religious motives. It is so much easier to justify it when it appears under the guise of zeal and pious outrage. If even Yahweh could become an enemy of his unfaithful people and punish them and make them suffer, is an Israelite's hatred for a heathen, or a dissident or a public sinner not justified also? The pathetic exhibition of his hatred for sin comes to be regarded as religious fervour and so the contest is on: who can voice the most blood-curdling curses? From simply keeping one's distance from the 'impure' or refusing to have dealings with a dissidents (e.g. Samaritans) or tearing one's robes in outrage at a blasphemer, they reach the extreme vengeance of stoning to death.

Christ, sign of the love of the Father

God in the Old Testament shows his love for man by his predilection for a particular people. He establishes a Covenant with it, he gives it a promised land, he leads it back there after various exiles. It is a story of tormented love. But in the fullness of time the love of the Father for mankind takes on a completely new expression in an unrepeatable gesture: his Son is 'sent' to be the protagonist on earth in the drama of this love-dialogue between God and man. This sending of the Son completes all the most loving gestures of the time of the promises . . . 'the promises God made, the "Yes" to them all is in him' (2 Cor. 1:20). 'In him, the love God has for us was made manifest' (Rom. 8:39). The initiative for this new order is exclusively divine and has no other explanation but love: 'God's love for us was revealed when God sent into the world his only Son. . . This is the love I mean: not our love for God but God's love for us when he sent his Son' (I John 4:9 sq.).

In this way the love of God is manifested no longer through actions alone but through a divine Person who, by the very act of his Incarnation in the nature of man, shows concretely the heights of this love. In Christ, God loves man infinitely and is loved by him. That is why Christ proves the genuineness of his being sent by the Father, not so much by his omnipotence, his signs, or his omniscience, as by his radically new concept of love which he comes to promulgate and to exemplify. The qualitative leap from the love enjoined in the Old Testament to the love envisioned by Christ affects love of God as well as love of one's neighbour. Through the revelation of his divine nature and through the acceptance of his supreme sacrifice, Christ opens man's eyes to the reality of God's infinite and pure love which to redeem us and return us to our former estate as his sons: 'did not spare his own Son, but offered him for all of us' (Rom. 8:32). 'Christ . . . loved us and gave himself up in our place' (Eph. 5:2). It is a love which is related to the Covenant established in the Old Testament only in as much as it is the consummation of the promise.

In reference to fraternal love and universal charity, the qualitative leap introduced by Christ is equally unprecedented. The novelty consists in the cancellation of all restrictions in the concept of neighbour and in the heightening and sublimation of the motive for charity. That the exterior acts by which this charity is expressed must be of unrestricted generosity is an obvious consequence. But before analysing these concepts it will be well to call attention to two fundamental considerations.

Christ is bearer of the Father's love

The first point to consider is the clear consciousness that Jesus has of the original character of the love he promulgates. He is fully aware that by so doing he is transcending the law and the prophets and is declaring his messianic role. In the doctrinal summary which Matthew gives in Chapters 5 to 7 of his Gospel, no less than six times Jesus introduces his preceptive teaching with a formula brimming with meaning: 'You have learnt how it was said to our ancestors. . . But I say this to you . . .' (Mt. 5:21, 27, 31, 33, 38, 43). There is no doubt that, however much this striking repetition can be ascribed to Semitic taste, it is also the true echo of the emphatic will of Christ that he be understood regarding the novel character of his doctrine and that, effectively, he is placing himself above the law. Three of the precepts thus solemnly promulgated concern charity. The striking attitude Christ shows in this connection is paralleled only by his vehemence in abolishing divorce. When Christ at the end of his life will have fully revealed at its deepest level all his understanding of love, he will affirm unequivocally that this is a 'new' commandment (Jn. 13:14) as is also 'new' the Covenant sealed with his blood which will be shed for us (Lk. 22:20) as the supreme pledge of his love. So unexpected is this novelty that at the beginning of his preaching his hearers exclaimed 'What is this? This is a new doctrine with authority behind it' (Mk. 1:27). Love is the most radiant novelty of the Gospel: it is pre-eminently the commandment which the Lord chose to call 'mine' (Jn. 15:12).

Only one love

The second consideration is this: The reason for loving one's neighbour is a theological reason which closely relates it to the love of God. They are not two parallel loves, nor is love of neighbour a subordinate love. It is the two sides of one love, as one is the love within the Trinity and one the love with which Christ loves the Father and mankind. The close connection of the second commandment to the first (as we shall see later, in Paul's and John's description where it acquires its highest expression) conforms to this profound causality: one cannot love God without loving one's brother and he, who for God loves his brothers, is already loving God (cf. Mk. 5:45 and Lk. 6:35).

The three synoptics report instances when Christ likens love of neighbour to love of God. In Matthew (22:34-40) and in Mark (12:28-34), Christ answers the pharisee's provocative question and with a hint of challenge he blends both commandments into one. In Luke (10:25ff) it is a quibbling lawyer who has to respond to Christ's sparring question. The casuist links the precept in Deuteronomy (6:5) about the love of God with that of Leviticus. (19:8) about the love of one's neighbour — neighbour, of course, as the lawyer understands the word. To correct the notion, Jesus tells him the parable of the Good Samaritan.

Christ manifests his own love
Of nothing else did Christ speak so much as of love, with the exception perhaps of the Kingdom: 'the kingdom of Heaven is like . . .' But even the parables of the kingdom are set in a context of love. Love with all its harmonics — friendship, compassion, tolerance, benevolence, mercy, sadness, hope, joy, etc. — is enough to describe Christ in his inner self, in his heart. Christ calls his followers to goodness and love, sometimes directly, from the beatitudes right up to the sermon of the Last Supper; at other times indirectly and through sublime allegories; the Prodigal Son, the Lost Groat, the Stray Sheep and the whole cycle of the Good Shepherd parables. Christ 'goes about doing good' (Acts 10:38) and displays his miraculous power in 'signs' which are more often acts of kindness than proofs of his messiahship.

Love without bounds: universal
If the love which Christ practises and teaches is the radically new feature of the Gospel, as indicated earlier, it is because it formally suppresses and abolishes the limitations and restrictions which previously narrowed down the idea of love. We know that 'Love your neighbour as yourself' (Lv. 19:18) is already the second commandment in the Old Law. But one needs only to compare this text with the other in which the first commandment is

promulgated (Deut. 6:4-9), to appreciate the difference in emphasis between the two commandments. The concept of neighbour is vague. The fluctuating meaning of the Old Testament expressions — 'the other', 'the brother' — is an example of this vagueness. When the decalogue, promulgated in other texts (Exodus 20:2-17, and Deut. 5:6-12) is epitomized in a single sentence (Deut. 6:5), all mention of love of neighbour disappears: 'You shall love Yahweh your God with all your heart, with all your soul, with all your strength'. There is no mention of neighbour whatsoever.

Christ breaks down the fences of a restricted brotherhood, and this is his great revolution of love: universal salvation, universal filiation, universal brotherhood and universal love, are all correlative ideas logically connected and interchangeable. We will see that there is only one exception: the preference for the neediest.

But it is necessary to mention expressly the two most radical changes introduced by Christ in the notion of universal love. In this new vision no one at all is excluded, not even those falling within the two categories which the Law excepted and religiously set apart: the enemy and the sinner. The whole history of Israel is a struggle for survival. Hatred for one's enemy is even ranked as a religious sentiment and as such it is expressed even in the sacred books (Psalms 137, 139 etc.). Enmity toward a personal enemy, a thief and those who ensnare the just man, is lawful. It is already an advance in moderating revenge when it is stipulated that retaliation must not exceed the offence: 'You have learnt that it was said: "eye for eye and tooth for tooth", but I say this to you . . .' (Mk. 5:38; Lk. 6:27). Jesus is specific: 'Love your enemies, do good to those who hate you, bless those who curse you, pray for those who mistreat you'. This is one of the high points of the Gospel, because here we discover the essence of Christianity, unconditional fraternal love.

Jesus expressed his thoughts in semitic imagery: turn the other cheek, give your cloak as well as your tunic, go the extra mile. The conclusion of the test is of the highest importance because Jesus gives the reason for his precept: 'So that you will be sons of the heavenly Father, for he is kind even to the ungrateful and the wicked'. The image which Jesus gives us of the Father is no longer that of the God who inspires revenge but of a Father whose perfection is manifested in his mercy. All is contained and epitomized in this lofty exhortation: 'You must therefore be perfect just as your heavenly Father is perfect' (Mt. 5:48). What reversal of values could be imagined more radical than this? Now it is the enemy that has to be loved, and precisely because this is God's way.

Love of sinners

There is still more: one has to love God's enemy, the sinner. Scripture praised the hatred God shows toward idolatry, plunder, perjury, any kind of sin (cf. Deut. 12:31; Jer. 44:4; Zac. 8:17; Prov. 5:16) and consequently for the sinner who in a way is one with his sin, and can be chastised with an impure illness. The Israelite affirms his piety by hating sinners. And here is Jesus declaring he has come not for the just but for sinners (Mk. 2:17).

Taking his place in the line of teacher-prophets, John, as his forerunner, announces the Good News for sinners disposed to repent. In Jesus, denunciation of sin rivals his inexhaustible compassion for the sinner. Jesus causes scandal when he forgives the adulteress, when he speaks to the Samaritan woman, when he heals and pardons paralytics and the possessed, when he ignores legal impurity in order to share a meal with sinners. To describe the Father and himself, in the parables of the Prodigal Son and of the Good Shepherd, Jesus refers to his heart open to forgive. By his whole life and by his death he will confirm all he has preached. He will even call his betrayer, 'friend', and ask forgiveness for those who are crucifying him.

More than his parables it is Christ's life that launches this revolution of love. Samaritans, gentiles of Cana, Tyre or Sidon, officials of the Roman occupation, publicans, prostitutes, lepers, all have a place in his heart. To love sinners Christ throws down the barriers of legal impurities, of the sabbath observance, of religious discrimination, of the sacredness of temple offerings. Loving sinners, Christ strips hatred of its last pretext: religious zeal.

70

The supreme love of the heart of Christ

It might seem that nothing could be added to Christ's proclamation of universal love made at the beginning of his ministry, and of which his whole life has been a constant confirmation. All the aspects of love are illustrated: the love of God whom he taught us to call 'Father', the love of himself and the love of our brothers. But Christ reserved for the last hour — and this word can be taken in the Johannine sense — the deepest and most significant lesson of his pedagogy of love. As evening falls, the day before his passion, and time is running out, when he no longer needs to hold back from revealing the fullness of his heart, now that his disciples have been witnesses of his life and work and are soon to be witnesses of his sacrifice, Jesus discloses to them the wealth of sublime reasons on which his love for them is based and which must inspire the love they bear for each other.

'Love one another; just as I have loved you' (Jn. 13:34). With good reason Christ can describe this commandment as 'new', for new indeed is such an unimaginable reach of love. 'You must love your neighbour as yourself. I am Yahweh' (Lv. 19:18). The scope of pre-christian love, which could have been as an ideal, in this new light shows its inadequacy. 'As I have loved you'. This comparison is the ever-pressing goad that from that time onward urges each believer in Christ to strive to love his neighbour without reservations or hesitations. It is a goal to which we must aspire always, even though we know we shall never be able to reach it. Only 'through his Spirit for your inner self to grow strong . . . planted in love and built on love, will you . . . grasp the breadth and the length, the height and the depth of the love of Christ, which is beyond all knowledge' (Eph. 3:17-19).

'As I have loved you' contains the entire mystery of the Incarnation, the *kenosis* accepted as preparation for the Paschal Mystery, the gift of self in the Eucharist, the consummation of his sacrifice and his perpetual intercession before the Father. Jesus speaks as a man to that puny flock of fearful men, but his words echo the love of God. The ultimate clue to this love beyond belief will be his twofold standard.

Christ proclaims a new comparative standard of love and he will personally fulfil it, 'a man can have no greater love than to lay down his life for his friends' (Jn. 15:13). Less than a day before his death, these words are evidence of a supreme love; it is the measure of his love for them and thus the measure of love which they must have for each other. Love is measured by self-giving. Jesus faces death and accepts it, conscious of the fact that by his death he proclaims his love for all men. The disciples will eventually understand the full value of the comparison 'as I have loved you': dying for you.

The second standard is by appeal to a mystery, 'As the Father has loved me, so I have loved you' (Jn. 15:9). Christ will repeat this in nearly the same words a few moments later in the priestly prayer: 'I have loved them as you have loved me'. Words which must be received with a reverence beyond expression. The whole heart of Jesus pours itself out in this supreme confidence that surpasses any human measure, because it already points to the infinite love within the Trinity: the mutual love of Father and Son. But this is the measure of love to which we are urged: love one another as I have loved you: I have loved you as the Father loves me. The most radical innovation the Gospel offers, charity, is thus established in its ultimate expression. But, is it not an exaggeration? No, it is not. Quite the contrary. It is a deliberate and conscious affirmation which John once again puts on the lips of Jesus as the conclusion of the long discourse, just before the evangelist begins the story of the Passion: 'that the love with which you loved me may be in them, and so that I may be in them' (Jn. 17:26).

The insertion of the Father as the point of reference for the love between Christ and mankind at this peak moment of the revelation of love is extremely enlightening. The mission of Christ besides other things, is the revelation of the Father. For this reason it is important to establish that the Fatherhood is also exercised in love, love of the Son, and unmediated love of the Father for mankind. The same Father, whom Christ invoked in the agony in the Garden and on the Cross, the ultimate challenges in the test of his love, is also invoked in the proclamation of fraternal charity: 'The Father loves me, because I lay down my life in order to take it up again' (Jn. 10:17). The same Father who '. . . loved the world so much that he gave his only Son, so that everyone who believes in him may not be lost' (Jn. 3:16). Fraternal charity, lived as Christ teaches us, is a direct way to approach the Trinity.

Christ in our brothers

In love thus understood the unification of the two ancient precepts reaches its highest perfection. Now there is one and no more. The same charity that draws us to God must also bring us closer to our brothers. In them we must find God. Christ is in them, above all in the most needy, in the poor, in the little ones (Mt. 25:40). During his whole life Christ showed his predilection for them and following his example we too must give preference to them. If the discourse on love is reported at the end of John's Gospel just before Christ's passion, it is in the same sequence that Matthew's Gospel reports Christ's proclamation of his identification with the poor. it is as if he were going out of his way to make sure that the fact remains imprinted on our minds: 'in so far as you did this to one of the least of these brothers of mine (hungry, thirsty, naked, homeless, sick, oppressed) you did it to me' (Mt. 25:40-45). A love of God that does not find expression in love for mankind is always suspect. Because 'a man who does not love the brother that he can see cannot love God, whom he has never seen' (1 Jn. 4:20). John warns us in no uncertain terms that love of God which is not accompanied by love of neighbour is an illusion. His language, which in places is almost of a gnostic loftiness, becomes concrete and incisive when he asserts that such love would be inconsistent 'if a man who was rich enough in this world's goods saw that one of his brothers was in need, but closed his heart to him, how could the love of God be alive in him?' (1 Jn. 3:17). 'Closed his heart' means depriving him of the love and the sharing which love implies. Because there is no other word which points more directly to love than the word 'heart'.

Paul, after his conversion, will completely assimilate this doctrine. He is the author of the most beautiful hymn to the love of Christ (Rom. 8:31 ff), and of the vibrating eulogy of charity (1 Cor. 13). He is the promoter of mutual aid among the Churches.

Of this assistance, given in the name of love, he makes an instrument of unity when there is a threat of division between the Churches of the Jewish tradition and those burgeoning among the

Gentiles (Gal. 1:10; Rom. 15:26; 1 Cor. 16:1-4). Two whole chapters of his second letter to the Corinthians are dedicated to organizing, urging and giving meaning to the collection of voluntary offerings (2 Cor. 8 and 9). So impassioned is Paul's plea that, with a hyperbole, he goes so far as to claim that the whole law comes down to fraternal charity 'the whole law is contained in this one command: love your neighbour as yourself' (Gal. 5:14). It is the old formula of Leviticus, brief and incisive, reflecting its rabbinical origin, and it helps him to encourage the Churches of the diaspora to practise mutual love: 'Serve each other for love' (cf. the same urged in Rom. 13:9-10).

St James, with the semitic expressions which are peculiar to his style, more homiletic than epistolary, exalts the poor and severely chides the rich. Charity must be shown in works so that faith may not become fruitless.

Charity and fullness

It is clear that *pleroma* (fullness) is a fundamental concept in Paul's theology. Besides the fullness of the times, there is the fullness which dwells in Christ, and again the Church is the fullness of Christ. This great concept is seen throughout Paul's letters, above all in his more lyrical and syntactically more intricate passages, when his enthusiasm for Christ, for the Church or for a particular community inspires his genius for soaring expressions to convey his thought. In the idea which Paul has of the fullness of Christ and of the Church, love is a basic ingredient. It is not only that love is the dominant theme in the whole divine plan of salvation — that which establishes the harmony of its different aspects — but the fullness of Christ, in whom the Father has placed all things, and the fullness of the Church as mystical body of Christ are one. Before the world was made, he chose us, chose us in Christ, to be holy and spotless, and to live through love in his presence' (Eph. 1:4). It is the love of God which chooses us and to this love corresponds 'the love we have for God that has been poured into our hearts by the Spirit which has been given us' (Rom. 5:5). Theologically and anthropologically speaking, the lyrical lift of Paul's hymn to charity (1 Cor. 13) marvellously heightens the sweeping novelty of the Gospel, the manifestation of the love of Christ's heart which establishes new relationships between God and man and between man and man.

John expounds the same doctrine. He takes it directly from Christ's lips when at the Last Supper Jesus proclaims his love for us and says that his love is to be the gauge of the love the brethren must have for each other. It seems he is acquitting himself of the last responsibility left before his mission is definitively accomplished: 'I have told you this so that my own joy', (this is the messianic joy of the Son of God) 'may be in you and your joy be complete' (Jn. 15:11); 'while still in the world I have told you these things to share my joy with you to the full' (Jn. 17:13). The fullness of joy of Jesus of which John was a witness is also a sentiment that John repeatedly made his own when he communicated his testimony: 'We are writing this to you to make our own joy complete' (1 Jn. 1:4). John knows that brothers' love for each other fills Christ's heart with joy and that sharing in this joy and generating it in the hearts of those who believe in him is a pre-announcement of the fullness of fruition that those in the Kingdom will enjoy when they will be assumed into the glory of the Father and their human love will be anchored in the infinite love of the Trinity.

There, one will experience that 'God is love, and everyone who loves . . . because God is love . . . is begotten by God and knows God' (1 Jn. 4:8, 16). To be of God and to know God in John's language, is a way of being possessed by him and of possessing him. Human love has its point of origin and destiny in the love of the Trinity. There is no higher summit that this.

It is now twenty centuries since the promulgation of the one and only commandment of love, a commandment that continues to urge us. Fraternal love continues to be a necessity for all men and for all times, and still more necessary in our time, now that the world has become a 'global village' and human interchange is on a truly universal scale. Universal brotherhood is no longer a qualitative aspect of love, in the sense of excluding prerequisites. It is a quantitative reality since the revolution brought on by communications, technology, and the possibility of exchanging resources. Because of this we can no longer plead ignorance of the miseries of our brothers in any part of the world; we can no longer say that they are no responsibility of ours.

All the modern tragedies are ultimately a wounding of love or a challenge to our capacity to love. The tragic fratricidal hatred of Cain for Abel is still casting its shadow over us: 'This is the message as you heard it from the beginning, that we are to love one another; not to be like Cain, who belonged to the Evil One and cut his brother's throat' (1 Jn. 3:11, 12), but 'this has taught us love, that Jesus gave up his life for us; and we, too, ought to give up our lives for our brothers' (ibid. 16).

The Danger of the Old Division

For this reason we cannot but decry the emergence of the old Jewish dichotomy which traced a boundary line between love of God and love of one's neighbour; a dissociation *contra naturam* that the Heart of Christ wanted to remedy for all time. It would be going back on the Gospel. We have not true and full love of God if we do not also manifest it toward our brothers, concretely toward those in whom Christ said we should recognize him. Nor have we true and full love of our brothers if in them we fail to see and recognize God and so reduce charity to the level of philanthrophy, robbing it of its transcendental dimension. Any of these failings wuld mean forgetting that 'the fundamental law of human perfection, and consequently of the transformation of the world, is the new commandment of love' *(Gaudium et Spes 38; Cf. also, 24)*. All the excesses of a reductive horizontalism or an unincarnate verticalism are an option between the 'first and principal commandment' and the 'second which is equal to the first' which after the discourse at the Last Supper no longer makes sense. They are a fatal corruption of the model of love proclaimed by Christ.

And unfortunately this is the way one could summarize the theoretical ends of the diverging lines of current thought and of Christian action. One must not so exalt Jesus the man — the person who had a predilection for the poor and the simple, who argued for detachment from worldly goods, who was persecuted by the religious and civic structures of his time — that one disregards Christ, the Son of the Father, who came into this world to save us all from sin, to infuse into our hearts the love of the Father and to give us the certainty of future life. Neither must one centre one's attention on the primacy of faith, on grace, and on the spiritual nature of the Kingdom to such an extent that one does not hear with all due senstivity the cry of the poor, and does not realize what existential human miseries so often challenge fraternal love. So the attitudes are typical of a harmful reductivism. Jesus is indeed the ideal model of a 'man for others' who was deeply pained when it happened that his hearers went without eating for three days in order to follow him. (How his heart would suffer today in the face of the widespread and persistent phenomenon of hunger!). But he is above all else, Jesus Christ, who 'loves us and has washed away our sins with his blood' (Rev. 1:5).

Experience and Knowledge of Christ
The cause of this dichotomy, or to put it in more pragmatic terms, of this meaningless fragmentation of the Christ of the Gospels is certainly the fact that we are not fully aware through experience and knowledge of the many facets of 'the love of God which has been poured into our hearts by the Holy Spirit given us' (Rom. 5:5). Our heart is in danger of continuing to be 'hardened' like that of Israel under the Covenant. We need that 'circumcision of heart' (Rom. 2:29) that frees us from the old Covenant of subjection so that we can enter into the new Covenant of love. Only this awareness and lived experience of Christ, in faith and charity, will enable us to present to our brothers Christ whole and not mutilated. We can do this only if we have obtained 'the spirit of wisdom and perception of what is revealed, to bring |us| to full knowledge of him who enlightens the eyes of |our| mind . . .' (Eph. 1:17-18). Only from him, in whom abides the fullness of divine life — and not from theorists or from any power of this world — can we receive that life and lead our brothers to the fullness of the whole Christ, which is the Church.

A well-known saying of Karl Barth is: 'Tell me what your Christology is and I will tell you who you are'. The idea we have formed of Christ — not to raise problems or to argue or debate, but only to feel his presence and love him, to seek him and find him —

determines our relationship to God and our Christian relationship with man and the world. Of the utmost importance, therefore, is the response that each of us gives interiorly to the question Jesus put to those who were about to follow him: 'Whom do people say the Son of Man is?' (Mt. 16:13). The whole history of the Church, its whole present state and the whole future of the Kingdom await the response we will give, both collectively and individually. A response which no doubt, in its countless valid formulations serves as a basis for fraternal dialogue, for mutual enrichment, and for the fuller understanding of Christ's inner self, his Heart.

Christ is God among men, and the Son of Man before God. He is the bridge that spans all chasms and therefore he is the only mediator. He is the sacrament of God in the world and therefore he is our justification. He is the Word that comes from the Father and returns to him, and therefore he is the key to all creation. His Incarnation and his revelation have made it possible for us to answer the question 'whom do men say I am?' But it is necessary to accept and live his word about himself if it is to grow in us, reproducing the Trinitarian love that confounds all logic: the miracle of love that is a scandal to the Jews, madness to the Gentiles and a thing of no account to the unbelievers of our time.

It is paradoxical that we should be more disposed to accept Jesus who suffers than Jesus who loves, and that in our brothers, we make the inevitability of suffering an excuse for our egoism and our rejection of love. There is a subtle temptation to accept Jesus the man and to be reserved with Jesus the God. It is urgent that we reveal to the world precisely this Son of God made man, without watering down the mystery. To proclaim the fullness of this love whose beneficiary is all mankind, each man, the whole human race, is to give the world a point of vantage for the realization of the *pleroma*, of the fullness of Christ in all things (Eph. 1:10).

Christ cannot be fully understood except in terms of his divinity: this is the essence of our faith in him. For the free gift which he makes of himself there must be a corresponding freedom in man to accept him. Both God's offering to man and the highest response of man to God coincide in Christ. I believe this is the reply we must give to modern conventionalism which speaks of 'Christology from below' or ascending, and 'Christology from above' or descending. Christ is the meeting point and very specifically we mean *the* point where the reciprocal love between God and man is consummated. Christology from below or above is a distinction which, in the profusion of current Christologies, can offer some methodological advantages. However, we must handle it with extreme care and avoid exceeding definite limits. Otherwise we will cause division in something which cannot be divided. Christ who came down from Heaven, is the same Christ who, having completed the Paschal Mystery, is at the right hand of the Father. Our knowledge and experience of his Person cannot be derived only from the 'Word' taken as the point of departure, nor only from the historical Jesus of Nazareth. It is dangerous to think one can theologize starting exclusively from Jesus to arrive at knowledge of Christ, or starting from Christ to arrive at a knowledge of Jesus.

A mention of Teilhard de Chardin is inevitable in this context. He saw Christ Jesus as the single focal point of the universe. Of course, we need not be in agreement with each and every step of his line of reason. But I mention him here because he inspires respect as the scholar who made the most honest scientific reflection compatible with an exceptional spiritual perceptivity and responsiveness. Teilhard professed an impassioned attachment to the heart of Christ, and on two levels. One, a pure and simple devotion to the heart of Jesus, along the lines of the typical presentation of this devotion at the end of the 19th and beginning of the 20th century. This he professed openly and without reserve. It is the heart of Jesus, which, in his spiritual life, is his standby in the extraordinary difficulties which he encountered in his activities as a scientist. It is the Sacred Heart of his diary, of his correspondence and of spiritual direction. The other level — and perhaps this division would irritate Teilhard — is that of Christ the *omega point* of the universe, whom he instinctively knows and who can be defined tentatively only in an act of love. Starting from the conviction that the universe is evolving and that each stage is significant only in terms of its relationship to the preceding stages, Teilhard concludes that the process as a whole must have a reason and an end, one *omega point* which is already virtually contained in the process itself and directs it from within, providing its dynamism and meaning. A few months before his death in 1951 he writes in his diary a sentence which indisputably reveals the final stage of his thought: 'The great secret, the great mystery: there is a heart in the world (fact of reflection), and this heart is the Heart of Christ (fact of revelation). This mystery has two stages: the centre of convergence (the universe concentrates in one centre), and the Christian centre (this centre is the heart of Christ). Perhaps I am the only man who says this. But I am convinced this expresses what each man, each Christian feels' (Journal, Cahier VI, p. 106).

Heart of Christ, Approach to the Trinity
In these pages the word love has been used deliberately more than the word charity, even though some people would reserve the word 'love' for the relations within the Trinity, and would prefer charity as more appropriate for fraternal love. Love has a more general connotation.

Apart from the fact that it renders better and, it seems, more scientifically the term and also the biblical concept, the analogy is diminished a little when one speaks of the affective relationships within the Trinity and those which exist among men. We start from the fact that through grace we are admitted to participation in the divine life, that is to say, to the intimacy of the Father and the Son in the Spirit. The philosophic terms that we apply to the Trinity, (nature, persons, relations) leave the mystery intact and must cede their place to the word: love: 'God is love' (1 Jn. 4:16). We accept that we cannot understand the mystery though we know that through love we are included in it: the Father and Son assume us in the Spirit making us partakers to the full of their love. Those who have accepted the mystery of Christ, says St John, 'will live in the Son and in the Father; and what is promised to you by his own promise is eternal life' (1 Jn. 2:24-25). This is possible in virtue of the love 'that God has poured into our hearts through the Spirit which has been given us' (Rom. 5:5).

But love, when defined, not by its object, but by the interior disposition of the one who loves, can only be one. That is why supernatural love for one's neighbour, whom Christ loves, and whom we love for Christ's sake, is a way to draw near to the

Trinity. Love of neighbour therefore, and not only of God, is a theological virtue. Especially for those who have consecrated their lives to the service of others following the evangelical counsels which have no other foundation but love; it is a way of direct access to the intimacy of the Trinity.

Is this not what we mean by contemplatives in action? It is not only a matter of an intellectural approach and intentional reference of our activities to the Lord. It is also to love him through our works and in all things (the expression is Ignatian but the concept is authentically Pauline) especially our brothers, since both contemplation and action have for their cause and end the one God, who is love and who commands us to love. The clarity with which we see God — and love him — in our neighbour is the measure of our spiritual coherence. This is 'the illumination of the eyes of the heart' (Eph. 1:8); this is the highest test that 'God's seed remains in us and is living' (1 Jn. 3:19). This divine 'seed' is nothing else but the principle of life, the Spirit who is at the same time, the personification and fruit of love. We turn to man and we find God. It is the theological sublimation of our fraternal relationship.

Whoever lives in this light of undivided love for God and man is not afraid to go forth into the world, because men will not be an occasion to interrupt his dialogue with God. On the contrary, they are so many more occasions for his encounter with God. Still more, in today's world characterized by unbelief, peopled by men and women who are not aware that they are the centre of the love of the Trinity, or who deny it, one discovers God through the great vacuum that their ignorance or neglect has left in their hearts.

The love which takes us to the Trinity is the foundation and strength of our community bonds. Our community has meaning only if we live in love. It is the love Christ had and has for each of us that has brought us together. Christ loves us individually, yes, but also as a group. It is the personal response of each of us to this love of Christ and the union of all these responses put together that causally establishes our group. As long as we are and remain united by him and for him, he is in our midst. Our plurality reproduces the plurality of Trinitarian love, which is all self-giving participation and communion. More than the community of faith — although it is that too — it is the community of love or, if one prefers, the community of love that is born from the community of faith, that constitutes the formal element of a fraternal community. This is the deep meaning of the joyful exaltation of togetherness which Psalm 133 expresses: 'How good, how delightful it is for all to live together like brothers'. It is an old experience of the Christian community that is renewed in us, that of being 'of one heart and one mind' (Acts 4:32). He who gives, reproduces in himself the generosity of the Father; he who receives reflects the submissiveness and docility of the Son, the bond of theological love that unites us bears the mark of the Spirit.

All that we have said of the Trinity, of love . . . is full of anthropological references. Is it not possible to express ourselves in any other way? Faced with this mysterty our minds are brought to a halt; the only entry is by way of the heart. And we enter into it more deeply and more vitally when our hearts are attuned to the Heart of Christ. This is, after all, what is expressed by the ancient prayer which the author of the Book of Chronicles puts on David's lips. 'O Lord, God of our ancestors, of Abraham, of Isaac, of Israel, watch over this forever, shape the purpose of your people's heart, and direct their hearts to you' (2 Chron. 29:18).

PART 3

PASTORAL
ORIENTATIONS

JESUS CHRIST IS EVERYTHING

*In his conversations with Jean-Claude Dietsch,
recently published in Paris (1982), Pedro Arrupe
explains in simple terms the origins of his devotion to
the Sacred Heart, and what this has meant throughout
his long and varied pastoral experience, both inside
and outside the Society.*

Jean-Claude Dietsch: *Following these deep and significant
reminiscences, I must ask you: who, for you, is Jesus Christ?*

Pedro Arrupe: I was suddenly asked this same question in the
middle of an interview I was doing for Italian Television five years
ago. The question took me by surprise, and I replied quite
spontaneously: 'For me, Christ is Everything'. And today I would
still give the same answer, but with even more emphasis and
force; 'For me, Jesus Christ is all things'. That is how I would define
what Christ represents in my life: Everything!

He was and is my ideal since the day I entered the Society; he
was and still is my way; he was and always will be my strength. I
don't have to explain the meaning of this in great detail, simply to
say that if Christ were removed from my life, it would collapse like
a body without skeleton, heart or head.

Jean-Claude: *Do you think that you already possessed some of the elements of this great ideal before entering the Society?*

Pedro Arrupe: Without doubt; although still in embryonic form. By means of the Eucharist — especially the devotion to the Sacred Heart — my father and mother tended that seed which was to flourish later on within the Society. Or, to put it another way, that which was sown by the Sacred Heart by way of my parents, was later cultivated and refined by the Society.

Jean-Claude: *The figure of Jesus Christ is a very complex one. Which aspects of it have affected you most?*

Pedro Arrupe: In some ways the figure of Christ does indeed seem very complex, or rather, presents many different aspects. But in fact it is very simple: whether Christ appears as a weak, helpless child or as the All-powerful; whether he is affectionate and tender towards the children or strict and severe towards the Pharisees . . . it is all united in, and proceeding from, one same root, which is love — this is where the figure of Christ gains its perfect unity and greatest splendour. What was a basic intuition for me as a novice has grown richer day by day, it has grown more vital. And the Heart of Jesus, as the symbol of this love, sustains me in my life and gives me the key to understanding the Lord without difficulty.

And so, this love gives life to everything else; for me, Jesus is a friend, especially in the Eucharist. My thoughts and deeds are nourished by Mass and by prayers before the Tabernacle. This explains why I am so amazed at the ideas of those who turn away from Mass and the Tabernacle and who try to justify this attitude by their theological ramblings! I should like to see St Ignatius listening to such ideas! What riches are lost by those who do not understand what Mass means in itself, nor what it meant for St Ignatius, and for so many Jesuits (both great theologians and simple brothers) who have penetrated deeply into his holy intuition.

We must always insist on this fundamental truth — that Jesus Christ is the Word Incarnate; he is the Way of God; and, for us Jesuits, the answer to the prayer from Ignatius to Mary in the

Chapel at La Storta, near Rome: 'Guide me to your Son'. This is also the constant prayer of the Society: 'Mary, guide us to your Son'.

Jean-Claude: I understand that the Heart of Jesus, although it occupies such a fundamental and constant place in your life, is rarely mentioned in the numerous letters, addresses and lectures of your Generalship?

Pedro Arrupe: You're right. Ever since my noviatiate, I have always been convinced that in what we call 'Devotion to the Sacred Heart of Jesus' is contained a symbolic expression of the Ignatian spirit, and an extraordinarily efficient means of attaining personal perfection and apostolic vitality. I am still convinced of this.

Thus it may seem strange that during my Generalship, I spoke relatively little on this matter. It was, however, for a reason which we might call pastoral, especially in those matters directly relating to the Society. In the face of all the emotional, almost allergic reactions that even the phrase 'Sacred Heart' would produce a few years ago — a phenomenon which was due in part to certain exaggerations and displays of affectation — it seemed to me that it was necessary that a little time should elapse in order to allow this emotional, this understandable, but highly irrational loathing to disappear.

I always was, and still am, certain that such a valuable spirituality, which uses a symbol (Cf. Eph. 1:18) of such universal and human importance, and a word — 'heart' — which is a 'key' word in the language *(Urwort)*, would not be long in opening a new pathway for itself. Little by little the cult of the Sacred Heart of Jesus will be revalued, but without being forcefully or repeatedly imposed on people, which would only serve to exacerbate or reawaken the rejection of the '50's and '60's.

It may seem to us that this type of symbolism and expression of our faith is neither suited to nor a popular expression of religion for a people which is not well instructed, or even ignorant. The words of Jesus say completely the opposite: 'Bless you Father, for you have concealed these things from the wise and learned men, and have revealed them to the simple'. With the poor, the little men, is this not an excellent way to make ourselves like them by adopting their attitudes to the Lord? 'Truly I say to you; unless you become as little children you shall not enter into the Kingdom of Heaven' (Matt. 18:3). Those are the words of Christ, which could be translated thus: 'If you, as people (and as a Society) wish to gain the riches of the Kingdom and to strive for it properly, you must become like the poor whom you try to serve. You often say that the poor have taught you more than any book; therefore learn from them this obvious lesson: love Jesus Christ, and you will enter Heaven through the door of the simple love of his Heart'.

In Japan, I never hesitated to consecrate, at their own request, many religious communities to the Sacred Heart: I knew, as did they, that this is one of the best possible ways to draw closer to God the Father of all men.

Pedro Arrupe, 'Itinerary of a Jesuit'.
Interviews with Jean-Claude Dietsch for his paper, 'Le Centurion'
— 'The Interviews', Paris, 1982.

THE HEART OF JESUS IN FR. ARRUPE'S MISSIONARY LIFE

Extracts from 'I survived the Atomic Bomb and Memoirs'.

In his well-known book 'I survived the Atomic Bomb and Memoirs', Pedro Arrupe tells us the story of his first years of missionary life in Japan. From this book, we have selected a few passages which bear witness to his personal devotion to the Sacred Heart, and to the influence which this exercises over his pastoral actions.

As soon as I realised that I was becoming fluent in Japanese, I decided to begin some kind of concrete ministry on my own account. I had no idea where to begin, but then divine Providence showed me a path which I had no option but to follow.

One day when I was visiting the nuns from a convent in Tokyo, I no longer remember for what reason, they approached me and said, 'Father, we should like to dedicate this Convent to the Sacred Heart of Jesus, but we can't find a priest with the time to spare.'

'Don't worry, I'll do it for you'. They were delighted. 'When can you do it? Now would be fine. . . .' 'Give me time to prepare a ceremony in Japanese, and then we'll fix a date very soon!'.

And so it was. After a few days I arrived at the Convent on the date previously arranged with the Mother Superior with my dedication and a short address, only a couple of pages long. It was a simple ceremony, short and full of those delicate touches with which nuns give a special harmony to their relationship with the Lord.

This gave me an idea. Whilst I was in Tokyo, I could dedicate myself to consecrating families to the Sacred Heart of Jesus, which without breaking any new ground, for which I had insufficient Japanese in any case, would allow me to cement firmly what others before me had first set up. With none of the difficulties involved in clearing a new path, I could secure that the old ones remained open. I never regretted it. Beginning with the families which I knew personally, and continuing with those that contacted me in one way or another, there were finally more than one hundred homes officially dedicated to the Sacred Heart of Jesus.

The Wonders of Grace
There was no lack of those wonderful things which our Lord promised to whoever should dedicate themselves to him within the unit of the family. How many times did I feel the grace of conversion in those short moments of a complete surrender which would last forever! But often, as I walked barefoot on the 'tatamis' of the houses which I had come to dedicate, I met sullen faces showing their resistance to me.

There were many families in which the parents, or perhaps a widowed mother, were Catholic. Among the children, one would find that division which Christ sent upon the earth, even in the closest relationships. Some children were Catholic, some Buddhist, Shinto, or merely uninterested. It was only natural that such a distinctly Christian ceremony would inspire not just distrust, but loathing, in those members of the family who belonged to another faith. But when, in the silence of a deep faith which had to be expressed, we began to pray in the simple, generous and suggestive words of the dedication, when the emotion of the Catholics overflowed into silent tears or frank, unashamed weeping, then the indifferent ones would feel grace penetrating through the natural emotion of those new feelings in their fast-changing world, with all the supernatural power of that which is divine.

Fervent but mistaken pagans, protestants piercing Catholic families like a splinter of broken bone, unbelievers who had lost faith in their false gods, they were all feeling that the blessed promise of God — no less real for their ignorance of it — was more powerful than their obstinacy and ignorance. From passive spectators who could not avoid watching, many came to be fervent believers with the sure promise of an early baptism into Catholicism.

A Solution for Japan
All over the world, the dedication of families to the Sacred Heart of Jesus is a great work. But in Japan it was especially so. The great difficulty in Japan, apart from converting people, is keeping the faith despite the thousands of difficulties inherent in Japan's material advancement. A Hottentot convert is in no danger of being morally 'drowned' by reading pornographic novels which no one ever has nor ever will translate into his own language. His faith will not be placed in danger by exposure to an atheist philosophy (by that I mean the atheism which denies God and fights him, rather than just ignores him), because a philosophy book of this type could never come into his possession. He will never taste the poison of a cinema industry which murders the soul while the body enjoys the pleasures of a placid euthanasia. A Hottentot convert is already halfway to Heaven.

The Japanese, on the contrary, read everything, know everything, in the cinema they see everything, they are interested in everything . . . and as there is much more evil than good in the world, upon their recently converted souls — weighed down by a secularist, pagan tradition — upon their souls will fall all the mire of the 20th century which, having turned its back on God, has placed the idols of science and materialism on the altar which once carried the Golden Calf of the Israelites on Mount Sinai.

A Japanese boy or girl will easily keep the faith only if they have in their homes a counterweight to the paganism of the world which surrounds and often overwhelms them. However, alone and without the strength and self-sufficiency of long established faith, they have to fight like heroes; this is true especially amongst the intellectual classes. We have statistics which show that

Catholic students, studying outside a Catholic atmosphere in which they were converted, abandon the faith at the rate of thirty per cent. That is why the dedication of a family to the Sacred Heart of Jesus is of such great importance in the lives of these youngsters. For faith, religion is not the exclusive property of the 'Kyokai', or Church. It is something more intimate which also lives between the walls, however poor they may be, of the home.

And when, because of awkward hours of study or work, it seems almost impossible to find the doors of the missionary Chapel open, if the Sacred Heart of Christ is present in the home, there they will find the supernatural support and strength which they may not be able to find elsewhere.

Devotion to the Heart of Christ and the Japanese Soul

The two intimate factors of friendship and atonement which comprise devotion to the Sacred Heart of Jesus penetrate easily into the heart of a newly-baptized Japanese. It is more or less complex, and of course useless in principle, to surrender oneself to discourses and subtleties on the material and formal object of the faith, of whether our attention should be given to the Heart which symbolizes Christ, or to Christ symbolized in the heart.

A new convert would not, apart from very rare cases, have the capacity to understand deep debates on the abstruse problems of philosophy or theology. However, he would easily understand other and more human ideas which are more than sufficient for the early stages of his religious formation. The friendship which we owe to Christ our Friend who died for us, the atonement necessitated by our sins and those of others, the reciprocal love which God lavishes on us at all times, these are the things which seem obvious to him and which will produce in him admirable reactions. He will also find in these values a positive effort which the faith demands from us, as opposed to the more negative reaction which, at first sight, is predominant in the Decalogue.

Along with the 'Thou shall not' which precedes so many of the Commandments, we find the 'you will' of the positive gesture of surrender which is implicit in our relationship with the Sacred Heart of Christ. (You will find rest for your souls). And given this synchronization of 'yes' and 'no', they find a more conscious and complete Catholicism; because the 'no' contains an implicit desire for self-denial and thus for giving to Christ: that is why I give myself.

Discovering His Presence

When I was making my first observations on this subject, I remember that my attention was strongly caught by a pupil of mine who would spend hours on end kneeling in front of the Tabernacle. She would arrive in the Chapel, and walking with the peculiar silence of those who are used to walking barefoot and noiseless from childhood, she would get as close to the Lord as her respect would allow her, and there she would kneel, indifferent to all that surrounded her.

One day we met as she was leaving. We began to talk and little by little I turned the subject of our conversation towards her visits to the altar. At an opportune moment I asked her: 'What do you do for such a long time at the altar?' Without hesitation, as if she had thought out her reply long before, she answered, 'Nothing'. 'How do you mean, nothing?', I insisted. 'Do you think it is really possible to kneel there for so long and do nothing?'

The precision of my question, which removed all possibility of ambiguity, seemed to disconcert her a little. She was not prepared for this kind of interrogation, and she took longer in replying. At last, she opened her lips; — 'What do I do before Jesus *Sama*? Well . . . be there!' she explained. And she fell silent again. It would seem, to a superficial mind, that she had said very little. But in reality she had said everything. Into those few words was condensed the whole truth of all those endless hours spent near the altar. Hours of friendship. Hours of intimacy, in which nothing is asked and nothing is given. One is just there.

Unfortunately there are very few people who can understand the value of this just 'being' with Christ, since to be real, 'being' has to include a surrender to Christ at the altar which has no other object than 'being' — doing nothing, just keeping company — if one can really call this doing nothing.

Children Discover the Value of Sacrifice

At the same time as this, another incident happened in a neighbourhood missionary class which was attended by both

Christian children and those in the process of being converted. I explained to them the value of a sacrifice made for Christ and how it could be an atonement, and we set up a little cardboard box, which looked like a moneybox, so that the children could drop their offerings of good deeds into it.

One day, two children who faithfully attended all the lessons had a violent argument which ended with a total breakdown in diplomatic relations. Each of them went to an opposite corner of the room, and there they stayed all afternoon, with the sulky faces typical of angry children, saying not a word to each other. 'Shimpusama, Itsuo-san and Takeo-san have quarrelled', the other children told me.

'What has happened between them?' I asked with curiosity.

'Saa, Takeo-san is in a very bad mood — kimochi — today. He would get angry over anything'.

The admiring way they said Saa told me that, although the dispute had not become irreconcilably serious, they had all been upset by it. I became curious to see the result of the dispute, because there was a very special relationship between the two little boys.

Itsuo-san was eight years old; still only a very young child, but in the opinion of his family eight was old enough for him to walk around in the streets without anyone to accompany him. Takeo-san, on the other hand, a tiny little boy of five, had not reached such heights of independence, and he needed someone to go with him if he wanted to go more than a few hundred yards from his front door. As they both lived in the same block, Itsuo-san would pass by Takeo-san's house on his way to school and to the missionary classes, and the two little chaps would always arrive and leave together.

That afternoon they had a problem. They had quarrelled, it was getting late, and they had to go home. I, knowing all this, was waiting to see how they would manage to solve their conflict. The children were leaving one by one after affectionate farewells, and now there were only a few left, chatting happily — and the two opponents, still sulking.

Whilst I was chatting with the last few stragglers, I could see Itsuo-san uncertainly approaching little Takeo-san, and saying something to him which I could not hear from where I was watching. But it must have been friendly, because Takeo gave him his hand, without either of them saying another word. They left angrily, but after all they had left together, which was good enough, as little Takeo-san's problem was that he could not go home alone.

When all the children had left, I picked up the 'money-box' with its offerings, and before putting them aside with those from previous days so that we could burn them before the picture of the Sacred Heart on the last day of the Novena, I noticed one which was not signed like the rest, but whose contents gave away its author:

'It was for you that I made peace with Takeo-san, even though it was his fault and not mine. To give you consolation, I will take him home as if nothing has happened.'

It was written on a filthy bit of paper, the back of a used envelope — but the spiritual worth of its content was enormous! That tiny person of eight years old, who had heard in his home and at school that revenge was a masculine virtue, knew how to overcome the anger which was burning within him and offer peace, friendship, and the thing which his rival needed most, the help necessary to get home.

The marvels of grace, and the mysteries of human friendship. The guilty party had not had the courage to overcome the pride inherent in recognising that he was to blame. On the other hand Itsuo, with a surprising delicacy of conscience for a boy so young who had been so recently converted, had that trait of the Sacred Heart of Christ which leads to the humbling of self, to charity and to help for others. He was only eight years old, and he had grasped the essence of devotion to the Sacred Heart with all the perfection of a practised ascetic. He understood nothing of religious distinctions and niceties, but he knew that in humility lay the greatest proof of his love.

The Promise of the Heart of Jesus
Another case showing the supreme effectiveness of devotion to the Sacred Heart during my apostolate happened when I met a Japanese lady, mother of a son and a daughter, whose husband

was the only non-Catholic of the family. They were all three fervent Christians. He seemed totally indifferent, and allowed his family to practise their religion whilst personally regarding it with a coldness bordering on contempt.

One day the lady came to see me and ask me to dedicate her house to the Sacred Heart. She wanted the Lord to have complete dominion in her house, not only sanctifying more and more those who already believed, but also curing the blindness of the last member of the household who had not yet found the truth.

I agreed immediately. What more could I wish for? I had already dedicated so many houses in what had been virtually my first apostolic action in Japan. . . . However, there was one difficulty which we had to solve, a reef which we had to cross without foundering: the near-hostility with which the husband regarded an act of faith, which could almost be described as a public one in his own house.

So we had a meeting — *sodan* — where it was decided that we would fix the date of the dedication for a time when the mother would be alone in the house with her children.

It was not too difficult. This done, we waited for the appointed day to arrive. On that day, I came to the family's house, bringing with me the articles for the Japanese ceremony which I always used for 'dedications'. The lady came out to meet me. I had expected to see her looking happy, as this ceremony was what she had herself requested; but I found her in a state of extreme confusion. There had been a mistake in the timetable. 'Father' she greeted me in a panic, 'my husband is at home'. I too was taken aback. It seemed that all our plans had been for nothing, as it seemed most likely that we should not now be able to carry on with the 'dedication'. 'Would it be best for me to return some other day?' I asked, floundering in a sea of doubt. 'No, Father, I don't think so', she answered. 'I have been wanting to do this for so long now, and there has always been some kind of problem. I think that the best thing would be to do it in a room that he won't come into, but carefully so that he won't find out what we're doing.' 'As you wish', I replied, 'You have the final word'. 'Let's try our luck and trust to the Lord'.

We went into one of the rooms. We placed a picture of the Sacred Heart on one of the walls and without further solemnity, as the secrecy of the moment did not permit it, we knelt down in front of it, the two children, their mother, and I. I began to pray. I read the dedication sentence by sentence, slowly so that they could absorb its full meaning.

We had not quite finished when suddenly and unexpectedly the *fusama* which separated our room from the next one slid back, and on the threshold appeared the master of the house, looking most unlike his usual self. When I saw him come in I fell silent, and his wife and children were frightened of what might be the consequences of this interruption. He looked at the four of us for a moment, then, bursting into tears like a child, said these words: 'Father, I want you to baptize me'.

He said nothing more. He could not speak. He was transported by the grace of God which had worked on him in a way that could be called miraculous. All his resistance was gone, his hostility, his indifference. . . . It had all disappeared in the heat of that spiritual calling.

It was one more proof that the Heart of Christ will keep its promise 'to reign over those households that accept him as Lord'. And, further, it was a convincing example of the power of the combined prayers of the mother and the children, who were all fired with the common, deep desire of converting the father, the only 'straying' member of the family.

The Missionaries Dedicate Themselves

In that mysterious battle for the conquest of souls, we continually felt our human impotence. We could only place our hopes in God. Therefore, with redoubled faith, we dedicated to him our hopes and efforts. Individually, we had done it thousands of times already, but the day came when we all were convinced that if we were to garner more fruit from the far corners of our lives, we must be prepared to do it all together, as a community. With deep emotion all the Spanish missionaries knelt before the image of the Sacred Heart of Christ. There, remembering his promises of blessings and his desire for reciprocal love, we made our supplication in full confidence in his goodness.

In our dedication, we brought together the profundity of the theology and the most intimate aspects of its personal meaning. In the name of us all, in a quiet and serene voice, one of the Fathers read the following words:

'Dedication of the Mission of Yamaguchi to the Most Sacred Heart of Jesus: Lord, we are kneeling here at your feet, in the same place as St Francis Xavier did, his heart broken yet still full of faith in you.

'Lord, we ask that from this day on, this Mission should become in some special way the Mission of your Heart. Therefore today, from the depths of our souls, we surrender it completely to you.

'O Eternal King and Universal Lord, you who choose the weak to confound the strong, here we are, the weakest of the missionaries trying to win this region for you, this region that turned Xavier into a white-haired old man. Convinced of the uselessness of all human methods, and feeling the ineffectiveness of the ordinary methods of apostolate in this country which you have entrusted to us, we have no means other than your promises. Lord, we trust blindly in your word: "To all those who practise devotion to my Heart, I will give extraordinary success in their labours". And, as we need that extraordinary success, we promise to you today that we will be true apostles of your Heart, leading a life of perfect love and of atonement. Grant us, Lord, the grace that if we were to disappear completely, this Mission would at once become the true proof of the reality and effectiveness of your promises.

'We, on the other hand, before the divine Majesty, through the intercession of the Immaculate Virgin Mary, of Saint Joseph, of our Holy Father Ignatius, of the first Missionary of Yamaguchi, Saint Francis Xavier, and of all the apostolic Saints and Martyrs of Japan, promise that with your favour and help we will expend all our energy and our whole lives on this one aim: that all the souls which you have entrusted to us, and the whole world, shall know the endless riches of your Heart, and shall burn with your Love.'

And God heard us. Today, we can see what then we could only believe with inner faith; he came to us in ways which we could not comprehend with our merely human intellects, victims of immense limitations. He wished that our growing Mission should become like the mustard seed when it begins to grow. But for this to happen, as a reminder of his bloody Passion, he wished his loving and redeeming Providence to be accompanied by our disillusionments, our sufferings, and our fears. He wished to test our faith, as he did with Peter when he walked on the water. And to do that, before the glorious light of the era which was just dawning, we had to pass through a black, dark night like his 'night of sadness' and through total abandonment by our fellow men.

The external reply to our dedication was prison for me and deportation for Father Gonzales Gil. But, however, what appeared to be a step backwards in the field of our apostolic activities was in fact nothing more than the end of a hard time which was already reaching the first beginnings of a stage that would be not only easier but which would bring many more conversions; this is the stage which we are living in today.

Today we can speak of Christ without external interference or unfounded suspicions. 'Lord, your thoughts are not our thoughts; your ways are not our ways. . . .'

A DEVOTION FOR OUR TIMES

Homily, Rome, 1965

A month after his election as General of the Society (1965), Pedro Arrupe was invited to preside at Mass of the Feast of the Sacred Heart at the Church of the Gesù, Rome. In this homily, he reflects on certain doubts which arose at the time of the Council and during the thirty-first General Congregation, still in session; and he opens up new horizons with his sensitive ability to feel the 'vibrations' of the people of today.

His Holiness Pope Paul VI, who is our main interpreter of the wishes of our Lord, sent a letter last February to all his Bishops on the occasion of the second centenary of the liturgical feast of the Sacred Heart. I quote a few sentences which illustrate the thinking of the Pope:

'We wish to explain to all the faithful, as completely, and, in the most appropriate possible way that we can, the deep and hidden foundations of doctrine which demonstrate the infinite riches of the love of the Sacred Heart. . . .'

Today, in fact, we can see in some a tendency to disregard the doctrine of the Sacred Heart, or at least to regard it as less relevant to the needs and peoples of our times. But if we listen carefully to the words of the Pope, we will note that it is precisely for modern Catholics that the Pope underlines the importance of this doctrine.

Pius XII, repeating the words of the great Pope Leo XIII, called it 'a practice worthy of all esteem, in which can be found the widest and deepest remedy for all the ills which attack both nations and individuals in the world of today'. Pius XII had no doubt that in this devotion to the Sacred Heart could be found 'the epitome of our religion, and also the most perfect rule of life'. *(Haurietis Aquas).*

Christ is the Centre

Jesus, according to Saint Paul, is the centre of all creation (Col. 1:17-18); heaven, earth, sea, angels, men, Jesus is central to them all and, in consequence, everything is centred in Jesus. But looking deeper still, we see that in Christ himself there is something 'central' which unites all that exists in Christ; a centre towards which all points of the circumference converge; a centre from which all lines depart towards the periphery. This centre is his love, symbolized in his Heart.

For the Pope, the love of the Word is at the centre of his divine life, the love which also brought about the Incarnation. The Word made Jesus our Saviour, and made him take a heart of flesh like our own. Infinite love is found in a tiny human heart; it finds a home in a fleshly organ, a sensitive, affectionate heart.

When St Paul announced the great synthesis of his apostolate with the words: 'Caritas Christi urget nos' (2 Cor. 5:14), he was not referring principally to the love which Paul had for Christ, but rather the love which Christ had for him. The love of Christ had taken possession of his heart. Therefore, it was not Paul who was living, but rather Christ who was living in Paul, Christ who loved and suffered through him.

And the same thing happens to each member of the mystic Body of Christ who truly lives his faith; in him lives the love of Christ which continues loving God and men, which continues to work and to sacrifice itself. The centre of Christian life is still the Heart of Christ.

To Attain Unity

The following thoughts may help to convince us of the Pope's affirmation; that is to say, that devotion to the Sacred Heart of Jesus is of great importance today.

Today's world tends towards unity, with its national, European, continental and even worldwide associations. Pope Paul VI spoke in his 1964 Christmas message of the evils of class warfare which is so strongly prevalent in today's society. This is that party or factional spirit, which places in opposition the ideologies, practices, interests and organisations inherent in the basic fabric of society. On the one hand, these complex and widespread social phenomena unite men with common interests; on the other hand, they open unbridgeable chasms between the various classes of differing interests, and make a *raison d'être* out of their opposition, thus giving our society, which is highly evolved from the technical and economic point of view, a sad and bitter taste of hate and discord.

While all the aspirations of the human race to seek unity despite the barriers to it, (because we have a common origin, nature and rights), are profoundly Christian aspirations, yet they meet, and will always meet, with insuperable obstacles, until the catalyst of the love of Christ is present in all men. This love is what makes a man give himself to the community as a gift of brotherhood, and this love ensures that each man receives the gift of the others. Each one of us must overcome his egoism in order to aid the community with the strength of the Heart of Christ.

To Glorify God through Science

The world today needs the Heart of Christ in its great conquests in the field of technology. Those who invent new worlds for us are not necessarily wrong when they exult about their 'discoveries', but they are wrong when they try to separate science from God, when they separate the Creator from the beauty of a world created by him. When science and technology enter on this path, they only meet the displeasure of God.

Who will show us, poor men, made of dust, how to be humble, how to be truthful? The Heart of Jesus will, the Heart of him within whom lie 'all the riches of knowledge and science' (Col. 2:3) of him who also said: 'I do not seek my own glory . . . my teachings are not mine, but those of him who sent me' (Jn. 7:16).

Jesus the man, in whose hands were placed 'all power in heaven and on earth' (Matt. 28:18) and who humbled himself before the heavenly Father, gladly realized and admitted that everything he had, had been given to him.

It was not hard for Jesus to live for the glory of the Father alone, because his humility came from his Heart, in other words from his love of God. Following Jesus' steps along this path, man can safely continue with his discoveries; because by them he will glorify our heavenly Father, and will never turn his own inventions into instruments of hate or destruction.

To Gain an Endless Source of Power

The world of today, in other words our young people, live with the 'intoxication' of atomic forces; they are excited to think that they hold an almost limitless power in their hands. Well, my brothers, this is another reason for saying that today more than ever we need the Sacred Heart of Jesus to stay amongst us or return to us. The reason is precisely this; that we are living in the atomic age. We are like a crazy child waving a loaded gun around.

Journalists have recently been investigating one period of my life, when Providence ordained that I should be in that region hit by the Hiroshima bomb, and that I should escape unharmed. I remember how, when I was still vividly affected by the terrible impressions of that disaster, we were discussing the lethal effects of the bomb used and its possible consequences with some young people. . . . I remember that after the youngsters had reached a very pessimistic conclusion about it, an idea suddenly came to me which impressed them all deeply: 'When it comes down to it, my friends, in spite of everything, and even if the worst were to happen, we know that we possess a force even stronger than atomic power; we have the Heart of Christ. Even though atomic energy may be designed to destroy and atomise everything, in the love of Christ we have an invincible force which will destroy all evil and will unite all our souls in one central point, in his love and in the love of the Father'.

To Combat Depersonalization

Another part of contemporary life is those great masses of human beings spread throughout the world: all classified by computers, labelled according to their various capabilities and attributes . . . but despite all this, the individual is submerged in the mass. Although we loudly proclaim the importance of the individual today, it is this same individual that is trampled underfoot, filed away, reduced to anonymity worse than that of any common soldier.

We need to welcome Jesus Christ back into this anonymous world; we need him to greet each one of us, hold out the hand of friendship and say, 'Before the world ever existed, I knew you. . . . I loved you, you in particular, and I gave my life for you on the Cross'. The thought of this inspired St. Paul, led him to exclaim, 'He loved me, he gave himself to death for me' (Gal. 2:20). What more could any man ask for? Even though the world might ignore me, there is a God who knows I exist, who is thinking of me, and who loves me!

To Find True Freedom

People today have a tendency to avoid as much as possible any obstacle placed in their path by the law. They believe that independence is something sacred, something sweeter than any other prize. Frequently, young people want to disregard the rules of discipline, imposed from outside. They say that these rules are an obstacle to the full development of their own personalities.

If only it were true that the human spirit were strong enough to overcome our disorganised instincts. If only our emotions were always so under control that all we needed was very little help or outside discipline.

But, however that may be, we should remember the Sacred Heart of Jesus, and there we will find the secret of our whole personality linked intimately with our internal lives. We would do well to adopt as our sole aim that of St. Augustine: 'Love, and do as you will', but only if we have penetrated the Heart of Jesus so well, loving him to the point of total disregard for ourselves; loving him to the point of being able to give up everything else for his sake.

To Stand Firm in the Storm

The final great sickness of our world is instability. If we look around us, we can see that everything is in a state of fluctuation: inside and outside Europe, in the East and in the West. The stability of so many governments and parties is weak. The value of money is unstable. Business deals are insecure. The rate of supply and demand fluctuates. But all this is only a symptom; the world today lives in fear of the instability of its own ideals. The principles of law and social justice are weak and uncertain for many of those responsible for human and national development; the philosophical structures of thought and ideals are unstable, even sceptical and agnostic. And as a result, even within the Catholic community, we notice a certain vacillation, a certain lack of conviction in private and professional morality. There are even those who would wish to get rid of the rigidity of dogma.

Is not all this just one more sign that we really need Jesus today? Only he is constant, indestructible as stone, and around him everything wavers in instability. Our Saviour has always been able to say 'Yes' or 'No'; through Peter he continues to give the support of his words to weak human minds — flimsy boats on a stormy sea. We should give our spirits something stable to hold on to, with a knowledge that is as fresh and as young today and tomorrow as it was in the time of St Paul; the knowledge of the love of Jesus.

St Paul wanted to let his Christians know with a warm certainty that we would never lose the love that Christ has for us. Paul stressed in his Letter to the Ephesians, some of whom were pursuing strange and mysterious ideals, that there is only one real knowledge, which is greater than any other: knowledge of the love of Christ, upon which the stability of human philosophy and thought depends (Eph. 5:18). It is a limitless knowledge, because the love of Christ is infinite in depth, height, length and breadth; it is not limited by time or by people.

This, brothers, is where I ask you to direct your minds and especially your hearts. In the love of Christ we shall have stability in our lives; the joy of knowing that we are loved, and security on our pilgrim way. This, especially, if we follow in the footsteps of Jesus and are guided by her who is Mother of eternal Wisdom, Daughter of Love and Lady of the Wayside — Mary, his Mother and ours.

A RESPONSE OF FAITH AND LOVE

Homily, Rome, 1973

Including in his text a large number of references to the Bible, Pedro Arrupe invites his brother Jesuits to respond to the 'sign of love' of Jesus Christ with love and charity, as it is the truest expression of genuine devotion to the Sacred Heart of Christ.

The Holy Bible tells us in the book of Numbers that the Lord punished the Israelites with various plagues, one of which was especially terrible: the plague of serpents. Many men died of their bites. Moses interceded on behalf of the people, and on the instructions of God he made a serpent of bronze and placed it on top of a staff: 'and if the serpent bit any man, he would look on the bronze serpent and live' (Num. 21:9).

When Jesus was talking with Nicodemus he used this biblical fact as a term of comparison: 'And as Moses lifted up the serpent in the wilderness, so must the Son of Man be lifted up, that whoever believes in him may have eternal life. For God so loved the world that he gave his only Son, that whoever believes in him should not perish but have eternal life' (Jn. 3:14-16). And later on, a few days before the Easter when he was to be sacrificed, Jesus said to the crowd surrounding him: 'And I, when I am lifted up from the earth, will draw all men to myself'. (Jn. 12:32). It is this symbol of salvation, which the Book of Wisdom refers to: 'he who turned toward it was saved, not by what he saw, but by thee, the Saviour of all' (Wis. 16:7) and continues: 'and by this also thou didst convince our enemies that it is thou who deliverest from every evil (v. 8); . . . 'for thy mercy came to their help and healed them' (v. 10) . . . 'For thou hast power over life and death' (v. 13).

Zechariah is even more explicit: 'when they look on him whom they have pierced' (Zech. 12:10), inviting us to see in this 'the Only Son', 'the Firstborn', whose wounded side, St John tells us, is like a spring of Salvation: 'But one of the soldiers pierced his side with a spear, and at once there came out blood and water' (Jn. 19:34).

The figure of Christ crucified on earth with its wounded side has its roots in the Old Testament, and seems to summarize the Gospel of St. John. One could even say that it summarizes Christianity as a whole. More than any other symbol, in St John it demonstrates the redemptive vitality of the death of Christ. The open wound, from which flow blood and water, echoes an old Jewish symbol: the wound is a symbol of death (the sacrificial lamb), and the blood and water are symbols of life and fertility. The pierced heart is thus symbolic of the Paschal Lamb of the New Covenant. The Encyclical 'Haurietis Aquas' says: 'There is meaning for Christians throughout history in the words of the prophet Zechariah as St. John applies them to Christ crucified: they will see the one they pierced, (AAS XXXVIII (1956) p. 339). The same Encyclical continues, 'there is nothing to prevent us worshipping the Sacred Heart of Jesus, in so far as it is the most expressive symbol of that inexhaustable love with which the divine Redeemer still cherishes mankind'. (ibid. p. 336).

Standing before the Crucifix, deep in prayer, looking at 'the one they crucified' from whose side flow blood and water, we feel that he is saying to us what he told the Jews at the Feast of Tabernacles: 'Jesus stood up and proclaimed, "If any one thirst, let him come to me and drink. He who believes in me, as the scripture has said, out of his heart shall flow rivers of living water" ' (Jn. 7:37-38). Words which were perfectly clear to Jesus' audience, who saw in this 'living Water' the water which they drew from their wells to offer to the Lord along with the harvest of their fields. They are even clearer for us, we who know the dryness of our souls and who feel a spiritual thirst: 'My soul thirsts for God, the living God' (Psalm 42:2). Like the author of the Psalm, our dry hearts cry out to the Lord: 'I stretch out my hands to thee; my soul thirsts for thee like a parched land' (Psalm 143:6).

Response to Unbelief

Many people do not hear the call of Jesus: 'Let him who is thirsty come to me and drink'. Millions of human beings, distracted by life's successes and failures, its joys and sorrows, will never lift their gaze to the Crucifix even though they feel a burning thirst for perfection and happiness deep within their souls; and so they will never experience true happiness. History repeats itself, and just as in the time of Jesus, men 'though he had done so many signs before them, yet they did not believe in him' (Jn. 12:37). They neither believe in him nor accept his word; 'the light shines in the darkness, and the darkness did not comprehend it' (Jn. 1:5); nor his works, 'the world was made through him, yet the world knew him not' (Jn. 1:10); nor even his Person, 'he came to his own and his own received him not' (Jn. 1:18).

Christ's words may seem hard to men, as when he tells them of the mysteries of the Eucharist (Cf. Jn. 6:60); if they do seek him, they do so out of self-interest; 'you seek me, not because you saw signs, but because you ate your fill of the loaves' (Jn. 6:26); they may want to throw stones at him: 'The Jews took up stones again to stone him' (Jn. 10:31), and even kill him (John 12:23). It is with good reason that the Gospel of St John has been called 'the Gospel of unrecognised love' (Mollat), and it is indeed true that 'men loved darkness rather than light' (Jn. 3:19).

Here is found the problem of unbelief, of atheism and of secularization. The world refuses to lift its face to Christ on the Cross, that fearful figure, not knowing that it is there that it could find the fountain of living water that would satisfy its thirst.

Response to Faith

'If you are thirsty, come and drink', said Jesus. It is necessary to go to him in order to believe in him. No one can find Christ and not become completely involved with him. It happened to Nathaniel on his first meeting with Jesus: 'Rabbi, you are the Son of God! You are the King of Israel' (Jn. 1:49); it happened to the Samaritans: 'It is no longer because of your words that we believe, for we have heard |him| for ourselves and we know that this is indeed the Saviour of the world' (Jn. 4:42); it happened to Thomas: 'My Lord and my God' (Jn. 20:28); it happened to many others who went to Jesus and believed in him completely; 'And many came to him; and they said, "John did no sign, but everything that John said about this man was true." And many believed in him there' (Jn. 10:41-42).

And with true faith we can live according to the rules of that faith. In his second letter, John writes: 'I rejoiced greatly to find some of your children following the truth, just as we have been commanded by the Father (2 Jn. 4). Living 'in Christ' means living a life whose principal object is love: 'Whoever confesses that Jesus is the Son of God, God abides in him, and he in God. So we know and believe the love God has for us. God is love and he who abides in love abides in God, and God abides in him' (I Jn. 4:15-16). It is easy to see that this is not a merely intellectual concept, but that it is rather a way of embracing the truth with the whole of one's being, and becoming permeated with the truth. We also see that without the love which is expressed in life, one can never come to a true knowledge of God: 'He who does not love does not know God, for God is love (I Jn. 4:8). True faith and true surrender to Jesus therefore necessarily means loving one's neighbours: 'And this is his commandment, that we should believe in the name of his Son, Jesus Christ, and love one another just as he has commanded us' (I Jn. 3:23).

This is the central thinking behind the whole ethic and morality of the Gospel of St John. The faith with which we believe in the 'bleeding Heart' is false and meaningless if it does not inspire us to love others; for 'he who knows not love, knows not God'. It is interesting to see how St John proposes that loving one's fellow man is the natural extension of God's love for us. Throughout the Gospel, the love of Jesus runs like an undercurrent, and we can feel the love which John professes for Christ, although this love never appears as a commandment, it is not even mentioned, whilst on the other hand John constantly talks about loving one's brothers: 'Beloved, if God so loved us, we also ought to love one another' (I Jn. 4:11).

St John reduces Christianity to its simplest form: belief and love. 'The believer', as Spicq would say, 'is he who knows what love is, and gives himself up to it completely'. ('Agape in the New Testament', I, 313).

Devotion to The Heart of Christ

To summarize: we have here what is at once both the simplest and the most profound view of true devotion to the Sacred Heart. By reading this Gospel 'written from within and without' we can learn of those 'treasures of knowledge and science'; of him 'who being found in human form . . . humbled himself and became obedient unto death, even death on a Cross' (Phil. 2:8). Through contemplating and reading about this crucified figure with the wounded side, we will see in him the Son of God, 'Christ, in whom are hid all the treasures of wisdom and knowledge' (Col. 2:3). And, drawing closer to him, we will come to have that belief which, if it is a true belief, will urge us to act on it. This action will of course be loving God, but this is a love which will of necessity also manifest itself in love for our brothers.

If God's love is indeed so great that he sent us his only-begotten Son, (Jn. 3:16), our response to that love must be an absolute surrender to Christ and to our brothers: 'Therefore, be imitators of God, as beloved children. And walk in love, as Christ loved us and gave himself up for us, a fragrant offering and sacrifice to God' (Eph. 5:1-2). This is why Pope Pius XII could write that in the cult of the Sacred Heart 'is contained the summary of the whole faith, and also the most perfect way of life' (AAS XXXVI (1944), p. 220).

This life of love for Christ and for our fellow men is not only the most perfect expression of Christianity, but it also involves all the characteristics of the Spirit of God; it banishes fear: 'There is no fear in love, but perfect love casts out fear . . . he who fears is not perfected in love' (I Jn. 4:18); it removes anguish: '. . . I am writing this to you so that you may not sin; but if anyone does sin, we have an advocate with the Father, Jesus Christ, the righteous' (I Jn. 2:1); it increases trust: 'In this is love perfected with us that we may have confidence for the day of Judgement' (I Jn. 4:17); it is a source of joy: 'These things I have spoken to you, that my joy may be in you, and that your joy may be full' (Jn. 15:11); an expression of peace: 'Peace I leave with you: my peace I give to you. Let not your hearts be troubled, neither let them be afraid' (Jn. 14:27); and a proof of victory: 'Whatever is born of God, overcomes the world and this is the victory that overcomes the world, our faith' (I Jn. 5:4).

A FEAST OF SORROW OR JOY?

Homily, Rome, Holy Year, 1975

This homily, delivered by Fr Arrupe on the Feast of the Sacred Heart of Jesus, 1975, closely echoes Pope Paul VI's Apostolic Exhortation, published one month previously, on the theme, 'Christian Joy'. Here we have an implicit reply to certain sad aspects of a false devotion to the Sacred Heart.

Today is the Feast of the Sacred Heart. It is a feast which implies a note of pain, of sorrow, of the Cross; the wounded side of Jesus on the Cross; from his pierced Heart blood and water flowing intermingled; the symbol itself of Christ broken on the Cross and crowned with thorns; the invitation to atonement for the sins of Man and for his faithlessness to the infinite love of Christ. All of this lends the feast of the Heart of Jesus an aspect of guilt, of pain, and of suffering. However, in its deepest reality this is the Feast of Love, and Love signifies happiness, joy and contentment.

Feast of Pain and of Happiness
One might say, 'Yes'; but in Christ's case, love presupposes the Cross. Moreover, the flames which spring from the Heart of Jesus are flames of love, of infinite love, and in this love we find the true meaning of the feast of the Heart of Jesus. The mystery of redemption can only be fully understood in the light of this love;

just as God's infinite love is the only key to understanding the Paschal Mystery, a mystery which although presupposing the Cross, also presupposes the Resurrection and Eternal Glory. This is why Pope Paul VI says: 'The Paschal *Exsultet* sings of a mystery resolved beyond our prophetic hopes; through the joyful proclamation of the Resurrection, the very pain of man is transformed; whilst the fullness of his joy springs from the victory of Christ crucified, from his wounded Heart, from his glorified Body, and lights up the darkness of our souls'. (Pope Paul VI, Apostolic Exhortation *(Gaudete in Domino, III)*.

The Heart of Christ is the symbol of infinite love, of the human and the divine love which he shows us through the Holy Spirit who lives in us. The fruit of the Spirit is joy, a joy which has the capacity to turn everything into spiritual happiness (Rom. 14:17; Gal. 5:22); that joy which no one can take from the disciples of Jesus once they have known it (Jn. 16:3; Cf. 2 Cor. 1:4; 7:4-6).

Comparing the deep and intimate love of Christ with the joy which comes to us through the gifts of knowledge, intelligence and learning, and which ripens into joy through the Holy Spirit, we can see that it is a happiness which embraces our whole being. It gives us an intimate happiness, even in the midst of the tribulations of this world, as a foretaste or a token of the perfect, and therefore eternal, happiness of the Kingdom of Heaven.

The Cause of Our Joy
This personal joy, when felt in its full breadth and depth, shows itself as a *joie de vivre;* it is an experience lived in the light of our faith in him, 'for in him we live and move and have our being' (Acts 17:28). It is a feeling of being filled with God, which brings us to life and which lives in us through the Holy Trinity; it continually creates us anew, giving us irrefutable proof of his infinite love.

This joy also shows itself as a joy that had been chosen 'before the creation of the world' . . . by that special love which presupposed that choice for a privileged calling '. . . so that we should be holy . . . in his presence' (Eph. 1:4). It is the knowledge of having been the object of divine preference: 'you did not choose me, but I chose you' (Jn. 15:16), 'you are my friends', and above all it is knowledge, confirmed by the testimony of the Holy

Spirit, that 'we are children of God and if children then heirs, heirs of God and fellow heirs with Christ' (Rom. 8:16-17).

Now this secure happiness is solidly founded on the love and omnipotence of God: 'If God is for us, who is against us . . . who shall separate us from the love of Christ' (Rom. 8:31,35); and in the full knowledge that, even though a mother may forget her love for her child, 'yet I will not forget you' (Is. 49:15).

There is the joy of those who know that they possess all the fruits of faith, the riches of knowledge and the wisdom of God, for which it is worth selling everything else in order to gain this precious pearl. And that pearl is mine! In addition, there is the joy of being tools in God's hands, the joy of those who know that everything they have and are is the work of God, due to his constant, natural and supernatural choice and aid. Likewise there is the joy of working with God, of being his ministers and his instruments, especially sharing in that work of all works, of infinite love, which is the redemption of the world.

His friends experience still another joy, the joy of having been created for Eternity, called into a way of life, eternal life, to which we look forward with all the hope and nostalgia of a man returning to his native land, and where we will join 'with great joy' in the marriage of the Lamb. (Rev. 19:7-13). Our earthly life with all its inconsistency has its end in Eternity. We have the sure knowledge that our names are written in Heaven (Luke 10:20); that at the end of our days we can look forward to perfect, eternal happiness (Rev. 18:20; 19:1-4), because, there, 'God will wipe away all tears from their eyes' (Rev. 7:17).

To Overcome Our Difficulties

It is difficult to understand this joy in the midst of 'Great sorrows in our world' (Cf. Rev. 7:14). The only light which can illuminate us in the face of such is our faith, a living faith which refines our perceptions and helps us to realise this definitive, transcendental relationship at all times. The only force which can overcome the hard cudgel-blows of suffering and tribulation is the fire of the love of Christ. Thus, in the Heart of Christ we have the symbol and the key of this divine alchemy which changes suffering to joy, pain to happiness.

One thing is sure; the true joy of Christ is born out of love, and the path which leads to it is the Cross. This is difficult to understand, and even the Apostles, after all the time they had spent as students of our Lord, only came to understand it little by little. We can apply to ourselves what Christ said to his disciples: 'O foolish men, and slow of heart to believe all that the prophets have spoken. Was it not necessary that Christ should suffer these things and enter into his glory' (Lk. 24:25-26). But when they did understand at last, they felt an infectious and irresistible joy (Acts 2:4-11), a joy so great that 'they left the presence of the Council, rejoicing that they were counted worthy to suffer dishonour for the name of Jesus' (Acts 5:41; cf. 4:12).

Those who have a living faith feel the fullness of joy within themselves (Jn. 17:13). They live a happy and simple life; they live 'with glad and generous hearts' (Acts 2:46), and they communicate their joy to others by their words and deeds, or, as the deacon Philip did in Samaria, they begin 'to preach the Christ' (Acts 8:5) so that 'there was much joy in the city' (Acts 8:8); even in the sufferings of a prison: 'and the prisoners were listening to them'. (Acts 16:25).

The Mystery of this Feast
Only after reflecting on all this is it possible to understand completely the mystery of the feast of the Sacred Heart, which is a celebration of love and not, as I said, of pain and sadness. In reality, this pain and sadness, caused by our imperfect understanding of Christ's love, is transformed by that same love into true happiness and joy. Now we understand how St. Paul could say of the servants of the Lord, 'we are treated . . . as sorrowful, yet always rejoicing' (2 Cor. 6:10), and how they could feel 'overjoyed . . . with all their afflictions' (2 Cor. 7:14), and why, as he says to the Colossians: 'Now I rejoice in my sufferings for your sake' (Col. 1:24). A joy as great as this is an invitation to his followers to share in it with him.

All this leads us to assume a positive attitude to the suffering of the Cross, and our joy increases the more we share in Christ's sufferings and his Cross: 'Beloved, do not be surprised at the fiery ordeal which comes upon you to prove you, as though something strange were happening to you. But rejoice in so far as you share Christ's sufferings that you may also rejoice and be glad when his glory is revealed' (I Pet. 4:12-13). St James himself writes to his followers: 'Count it all joy, my brethren, when you meet various trials . . . the testing of your faith produces steadfastness' (Jas. 1:2-3). The key to all this is in the manner in which Christ himself considered his suffering and his Cross, who for the joy that was set before him endured the cross, despising the shame' (Heb. 12:2).

In conclusion, I should like to quote the words of Pope Paul VI: 'Throughout the course of this year, we believe we have followed faithfully the inspirations of the Holy Spirit, inviting all Christians to return to the source of joy' *(Gaudete in Domino)*. We need joy in today's world; there is already so much suffering, anguish and insecurity. The source of happiness is the Heart of Christ, the symbol of God's endless love, who '. . . so loved the world that he gave his only Son' (Jn. 3:16). Our happiness springs from this love, it is the secret which will transform everything into joyfulness, it is true happiness which can satisfy the hearts of men.

Those who know love in its deepest, transcendental form will feel it to be a 'flame of living love', a 'sweet song', a 'gentle feeling', with the taste of eternal life which 'in dying, death gives life in exchange'. (The Flame of Living Love: Canto 2a). Here is the secret of human happiness, hidden from the wise and learned men, only to be discovered by meek and humble men.

I pray that the Lord will grant that the feast of the Sacred Heart this year should show us a means of how to sing, from the bottom of our hearts and with the fullness of our joy, an endless 'Alleluia'. The suffering of the Cross will pass, but the joy of the eternal 'Alleluia' not only will not pass, but it will also be the prelude to a more perfect 'Alleluia', the heavenly 'Alleluia' sung by the blessed in heaven.

THE MYSTERY OF MERCIFUL LOVE

Homily at Rome, 1979

In advance of the publication of Pope John Paul II's great Encyclical, Dives in Misericordia, but based on other writings of the same Pope which had already been published, Fr Pedro Arrupe presents this homily on the Sacred Heart of Jesus as a supreme revelation of the mysteries of God and Man.

In all the languages of the world there are words that can be considered as basic, original words, 'source words', as opposed to other words which are called 'technical' or 'useful'. Those in the first category possess an enormous power of evocativeness; they are like sea-shells echoing the sounds of the sea. Those in the second category have been coined by men for practical or utilitarian purposes. The first type are full of the power of persuasion, they evoke deep and varied images and feelings, and often they have a different meaning for each man according to his own personal experience. The other type are simple, concrete words, used for ideas and things from our everyday lives, and never go further than concrete realities.

The words 'Heart of Jesus' is one of those 'source phrases'; it is basic, fundamental and original. 'Heart' is a complex concept whether we study it within the concepts of biblical theology, popular language, or everyday life. It has come to mean the entirety of a man, and is deeper than the philosophical distinction between biological body and incorporeal spirit. 'Heart' is a true symbol. It expresses the most basic centre of the psychological unity of a man; it is the intimate centre of each man in as much as it is here that the opening up to God and to other men essentially takes place.

The heart is like a consciousness of the origin of decisions. It is the 'I' of a man, his interior, his hidden personality, as opposed to his external image. In the heart is found everything that God placed in man; his law is engraved here, it is filled with the Holy Spirit, it is here that the Trinity resides. This is the intimate contact, *toto ictu cordis* of St Augustine and St Monica at Ostia: (Confess. IX, 10, n.23-25). For the Christian, the heart represents the source of his personal life, where thoughts, love and feelings form, as St Augustine said, one sole entity: 'cor meum ubi ego sum quicumque sum' (Confess. X, 3-4).

The Heart of Christ Reveals the Mysteries of God

The Heart of the Redeemer has an ever deeper meaning for us. The experience of our faith makes of it a symbol of the infinite love of our Saviour for his Father and for all men; it sums up the symbolic meaning of the Incarnation and of Salvation, which are God's works of love for us men.

In this way, the 'Heart of Christ' is like a pointer showing us where we must find our most profound faith; it is like a huge door which admits us so that we are able to understand better the mysteries of the Trinity and the *ad extra* works of God himself, who gives his love and his self to us. As we approach the understanding of this divine love, symbolized by the Sacred Heart of Jesus, we will find the supreme inspiration for living our lives as sons of God, and for gaining the deepest realization of so many of our basic desires.

The Heart of Jesus is a doorway to God. Guided by his only-begotten Son, we can approach the 'Holy, All-powerful and Eternal One' with profound reverence, so that he may reveal to us his mystery, 'which was kept secret for long ages, but is now disclosed' (Rom. 16:25-26). Although what St John of the Cross says is true, that 'the nearer the soul comes to God it perceives that darkness is greater and deeper because of its own weakness' (The Dark Night of the Soul, Bk. II, C. 16); however, from the midst of the darkness shines a light which helps us to penetrate its depths; it is a 'shining darkness' which shows us how to understand 'with a knowledge which transcends all knowledge'.

This mystery of love is the mystery of the life of the Holy Trinity, a life of communion and communication. Love, says St Ignatius, is a communication of what one has and what one is. (Cf. Spiritual Exercises, 231). This is what the Holy Trinity does. The Father begets the Son, fully communicating with him throughout all eternity the completeness of his divine Being, and the Son replies, also throughout eternity, by returning himself in full to the Father with all the impetus of his love. (John 1:1; I John 1:1-7). Here is the mystery of divine love, in which, as they are perfect Beings in themselves, they communicate fully by giving their own selves. This communication of love between Father and Son is so strong, so intimate, so profound, that in some way (a divine way!) it is itself a Being, in other words the Holy Spirit. Each one of the three has no separate existence, their Being is defined by each giving of himself completely to the Other Two at the same time and at all times. Each is a point of reference between the Other Two. Their whole Being is a pure, a complete, 'issuing forth' of themselves (an ecstasy), a yearning towards the Others, an 'irruption' towards the Others as the Greek Fathers would say.

The Heart of Christ Reveals the Mysteries of Man

In the light of God, the idea of what constitutes human perfection becomes clear to us. Modern psychology has 'rediscovered', in terms understandable to contemporary man, what scholastic theology was already teaching; our nature (with its organs and feelings) and our soul (with its faculties) can only grow, develop, ripen and reach fullness through a process of acquisition. We consume food, we observe concrete facts, we acquire certain abilities . . .; but our inner being, our most personal and intimate being, can only reach its fullness and perfection by following an opposite process. We develop personally in proportion as we are drawn out of ourselves, how we interact with others, how we serve them: 'It is more blessed to give than receive' (Acts 20:35), and, 'God loves a cheerful giver' (2 Cor. 9:7).

The Heart of Jesus is a door through which we can also discover God's *ad extra* works. If love always means communication, that infinite love which is God communicates outwards from him and, through Creation, he spreads his perfection through all the creatures in the universe, making them reflections of his own Light; but man in particular was created by God 'in his own image'; he was made capable of love, of communication, of giving fully of himself to others, and this is where the full realization of his human potential and happiness lies: (Acts 20,35). More, man wishes to make himself a part of that communion of love and life which we call the Trinity: (John 17:3,21). This is why God sent his Son to the world (Jn. 3:16-17). And Christ carries out his mission as Redeemer precisely through the total surrender of himself which even included death on the Cross. It is a surrender and an offering of love and obedience to God, and a surrender of his life to us, his brothers, giving us the capacity for this divine life in the measure in which we are capable of receiving it: 'I came that they may have life, and have it abundantly' (Jn. 10:10).

If we go deeper, and wish to discover the kind of love with which Jesus loves us, we must listen to his words: 'As the Father has loved me, so have I loved you' (Jn. 15:9). What does this mean? Jesus himself tells us at the Last Supper: 'that the love with which thou hast loved me may be in them |my disciples|, and I in them' (Jn. 17:26). It may seem impossible that Jesus could love us with the same love with which he is loved by his Father; however, as St John says, 'how can it be otherwise if we share in his divine nature?'

In this context Jesus continues: 'This is my commandment that you love one another as I have loved you' (Jn. 15:12). Christian love is, therefore, love of that kind which comes only from the Father and the Son: 'because God's love has been poured into our hearts through the Holy Spirit who has been given to us (Rom. 5:5). This is the perfect answer to our egoism; we will love with the same love which Christ shows for us, and which is a part of that one love of the Father and the Son.

The History of Love and Mercy
His Holiness Pope John Paul II defines this revelation of love as mercy, and says that 'this history of love and mercy has a shape and a name in the story of mankind: that name is Jesus Christ' (*Redemptor Hominis*, 2, p.9).

Thence comes compassion for all men, and especially those who are suffering; thence comes understanding of others, with the desire to be 'more ready to excuse the proposition of another than to condemn it' (Ex. Spir.) as St Ignatius teaches. It is in fact with this loving mercy that God desires the salvation of man: '. . . God our Saviour, who desires all men to be saved and to come to the knowledge of the truth' (I Tim. 2:3-4). In other words, God wants all men to become children of the Father; this gives a most profound meaning and a divine basis to the idea of apostolic zeal, with which one labours to ensure the acceptance of God's word by all men: this is the real motive of evangelization.

The Pope himself remarks on this in his Encyclical: 'Man cannot live without love. Without it he will forever be a being incomprehensible in himself. His life will be deprived of all sense if love doesn't reveal itself to him, if he never encounters love, if he doesn't experience it in some manner and make it part of his life or if he doesn't participate deeply in it'. Precisely by this love, concludes the Pope, 'Christ the Redeemer fully reveals the man to himself' (Red. Hom. n.10). This is why in order to be able to understand mankind completely, in other words, to penetrate the heart of man, that most profound and basic centre of which we spoke earlier, we have first to enter into the Heart of that God-Man, that same God who became man in order that all men should become truly men and sons of God.

It is only by entering through this door which is the Heart of Christ that we will be able to comprehend the grandeur and holiness of God, our worthiness of being sons of God in the deepest sense of our humanity, which is the basis of the equality between all men before God, who makes no 'distinction between men' (Eph. 6:9), and who died for all of us equally, for all men and women without distinction. We will also understand the value and the eternal repercussions of our complete surrender to others in brotherly love, wherein lies the perfection of mankind, and which impels us to collaborate in the Lord's plan of universal salvation: 'for we are God's fellow workers' (I Cor. 3:9).

This is how we should feel when Jesus Christ, the Redeemer of mankind, shows us his Heart and says to us: 'I am the door; if anyone enters by me, he will be saved, and will go in and out and find pasture' (Jn. 10:9).

TESTAMENT OF FR. PEDRO ARRUPE

From his Address: 'Rooted and Grounded in Love', 1981

On February 15th 1981, Fr Pedro Arrupe made his last great speech to the Society of Jesus, on the occasion of the closing of the Ignatian Course held in the Lecture Hall at Jesuit Headquarters in Rome. The speech is entitled 'Rooted and Grounded in Love', and in it he explains his theme of 'the centre of the Ignatian Experience'. The last part of the speech, which is the shortest and also the most intimate and personal part, was delivered with particular emphasis to an expectant and hushed audience. It is not just a résumé of his longer speech, but rather his true spiritual testament.

At this point, having already seen that love is the basis of Christian spirituality, and, therefore, also of Ignatian spirituality, I feel obliged to put forward one last consideration.

What has been said up to now can be summarized in five points:

(1)   Love (service) towards mankind, towards Christ, the Lord, constitutes a unique and indivisible object of our charity.

(2)   Love will resolve all the dichotomies and tensions which can occur within an imperfectly understood Ignatian Spirituality. For example:—

Tension between faith and justice is resolved by charity. Faith must be influenced by charity, 'fides informata caritate', and in this way the judgement arrived at will be of a superior justice: charity requires justice.

Tension between perfection of self and of others. Both must be the perfection of one and the same charity, which tends to grow constantly, as much intensively in itself as extensively in the increase and perfection of others.

Tension between preaching and active conversion is resolved by 'contemplativus in actione', by seeking God in all things (contemplation as a means to love).

Tension between the three religious vows disappears when it is based on and carried out in a state of mind moved and inspired by charity (this also applies to the fourth vow).

Tension between free choice and obedience. Charity must be present throughout the whole process of making free decisions: the presence of 'agape' allows the discernment of the will of God (Cf. Rom. 12:2); it is an intimation of charity (Eph. 3:18-19; Col. 2:2). Obedience, for its part, is the expression of this same will of God. The Superior, as much as his subjects, must be informed and motivated by charity, with its own intimation of love: (Therrier: 'Discernment in the Writings of St Paul', p. 179).

(3) Love is the solution for apostolic problems created by modern evils *(anomia)*.

(4) Love is the basis of all things, and it gives unity to the character and all the works of Jesus Christ.

(5) Love is also basic to our lives and activities, as there is that common spirit (the Being called Love) between Christ and ourselves, and which makes us call out as Christ did, 'Abba, Father'.

Therefore this, when understood in all its depth and breadth (love and mercy) is the résumé of the life of Jesus, and should also be the résumé of our lives as Jesuits.

Now, the natural symbol for love is the heart. Therefore, the Heart of Christ is the natural symbol representing and inspiring our own personal and institutional spirituality, carrying us with it to the source and the depths of the human-divine love of Jesus Christ.

A Contradiction: Love and Silence?

Therefore, as I come to the end of this address, I have something to say to the Society which I believe should be said.

Since my novitiate, I have always been convinced that what we call 'Devotion to the Sacred Heart' is a symbolic expression of the very basis of the Ignatian spirit, and an extraordinarily effective means — *ultra quam speraverint* — as much for gaining personal perfection as for apostolic success. I still have this conviction. It may have seemed strange to some of you that during my Generalship I should have spoken relatively little on this theme. I did have a reason for this, which we might call a pastoral reason. In recent years the very expression 'Sacred Heart' has constantly aroused, from some quarters, emotional, almost allergic reactions, perhaps in part as a reaction against certain means of presentation and terminologies more suited to the tastes of an earlier time. Therefore it seemed to me to be advisable to allow a little time to pass, in the certainty that this attitude, which is emotional rather than rational, should die down somewhat.

I have always entertained the conviction that the high value of this profound spirituality would not be long in reestablishing itself in the esteem of all. For it is a spirituality which successive Roman Pontiffs[1] have classed as 'a supreme spirituality'. It is, moreover one which makes use of a biblical symbol,[2] the heart, which itself is a 'source word' *(Urwort)*.

For this reason, and very much in spite of myself, I have spoken and written relatively little about this theme, although I have often dealt with in more personal conversations, and in this devotion I myself possess one of the deepest sources of vitality for my interior life.

---

1   Cf. Leo XIII "Annum Sacrum", 1899; Pius XI "Miserentissimus Redemptor, 1926; Pius XII "Haurietis Aquas", 1956; Paul VI "Investigabiles Divitias", 1965.

2   Eph. 1:18.

At the end of this series of conferences on the charisma of Ignatius, I could not but explain to the Society the reasons for this silence, which I hope you will understand. And at the same time, I have no wish to keep silence about my personal, profound conviction that all of us in this Society of Jesus should, before our crucifix, meditate and decide exactly what this devotion has meant and should mean today for the Society. In present circumstances, the world offers us challenges and opportunities which can only be solved with the strength of this love for the Heart of Christ.

Final Advice to the Society

This is the message which I want to share with you. It does not involve forcing things, nor ordering anything; for it is a matter into which each must enter by means of love. But I do say: think about it, and 'reflect on what it might offer'.[3] It would be very sad if, being in possession of such a great treasure for our personal and institutional spirituality, we should ignore it for unacceptable reasons.

If you want my advice, after fifty-three years as a Jesuit and nearly sixteen as General, I would say to you that in this devotion to the Heart of Christ can be found an enormous strength; it is for each one of us to discover it — if you have not discovered it already — and apply it to your personal lives in the way that our Lord showed and granted it to us. It is an extraordinary gift offered to us by God.

The Society has need today of the 'dynamism' incorporated in this symbol and in that reality which helps us to understand it — the love of the Sacred Heart of Christ. Perhaps what we need is an act of communal humility so that we might accept what the Supreme Pontiffs, the General Congregations and the Generals of the Society have always told us. However, I am of the belief that there are very few proofs of the spiritual renewal of the Society of Jesus that could be as clear as an efficacious and general renewal

---

3 Exercises: 53.

of devotion to the Sacred Heart. Our apostolate would receive new courage, and we would not be long in seeing the effects, as much in our own personal lives as in our apostolic activities.

We must not fall into the trap of deceiving ourselves about a devotion expressed by a symbol or by a graphic representation of that symbol. Let us not join with the clever and learned men of this world from whom our Father hides his mysterious truths whilst revealing them to those who become as little children.[4] Let us possess that simplicity of heart which is the prime condition for a profound conversion: 'if you do not become as little children. . . .[5] Those are words of Christ, which could be interpreted thus: 'If you, as individuals and as a Society, wish to enter the Kingdom of Heaven and help to build it with the greatest effectiveness, you must become like the poor people whom you wish to serve. How many times do you repeat that the poor have taught you more than many books? Learn from them this simple lesson, learn from my Heart of my Love'.

---

4   Luke 10:21; Matt. 11:25.
5   Matt. 18:3.

IN RETROSPECT

'. . . AND ALL THIS FOR ME . . .'

(Spir. Ex. 116)

That Christ is the stimulus in the life of Fr Pedro Arrupe and in all his writings is evident in the preceding texts and is proven in so many others, which even if Christ is not the main theme, can only be understood through Christ; through a Christ very personally lived with and 'internally felt'.

On the occasion of his fiftieth year in the Society (1977), I was requested to attempt to write a basic synthesis of the particular Christ of Fr Arrupe. I think that the following statements made then, retain their meaning and are appropriate at the end of this book, and may even confirm its message.

The Christ of Fr Arrupe

. . . Sometimes I have heard Jesuits discuss the Christology of Fr Arrupe. Is it classical, current, modern or an updated Christology? I think this is an unnecessary discussion, I would even say banal. I can certainly testify to having seen on the desk of the Father General (I must confess my curiosity) the books of most current Christologists of different tendencies, ranging from those of Schillebeeckx, Schoonenberg, Galot, to the most recent of the

Latin or Latin-American Christologies, Gonzalez and John Sobrino. . . .

But this is not important. What really interests the Society is not their Christology but their Christ; the Christ which Fr Arrupe lives, the Christ he proclaims and reports as 'having seen and heard'. What interests him is his personal 'knowledge', his personal experience of Christ. (I am well aware that from a psychological and sociological point of view, great reticence is demanded in relation to these 'experiences' of God which man lives and reports. Nevertheless it is the conviction of many people from Paul of Tarsus to Mother Teresa of Calcutta, that these experiences are so true that they affect life profoundly though they may be mysterious and intangible in themselves).

Therefore, we are interested in the particular manner by which Father General has been 'affected', 'touched', 'reached', (Phil. 3:12) by Jesus. It is something which is very difficult to express, but which produces effects, attitudes . . . shaping our daily lives, giving us that *sensus Christi* to which Father General frequently refers in his conversations and for the loss of which he expresses a deeper grief than for some of our other losses.

I proffer my excuses in advance if I have dared to describe very briefly this Christ of Fr Arrupe.

It is fundamentally and above all the Christ of St Ignatius of Loyola, with a personal tinge. We find it everywhere in all his writings. I beg leave to summarize those passages which I think are underlined more strongly and with greater frequency.

It is the Trinitarian Christ, with whom we are sent and through whom we approach the Father. Let us ask ourselves about the kind of approach, dialogue, union, the kind of docility to the Spirit of Christ that we try to have in our life. Beyond words, always by approximation, we need to rediscover a simple truth and from that draw all the conclusions; Christ is alive, he speaks and acts, receiving from the Father his being, his words, his action; and our existence or life develops within Christ, so that we are sharers in his relationship with the Father.

He is the Christ of the Incarnation and of the meditation on the Kingdom, Son and Envoy in the one Person, who takes unto himself tormented mankind and creates a new kind of man and world! 'The young will be helped to meet God . . . if they learn to contemplate the universal misery which is crying aloud for a Redeemer. The apostle will always respond to human misery. The Jesuit will profit greatly if with the freedom of humility and apostolic magnanimity he puts on Christ, accepting himself and all others . . .' (AR XV 115).

It is the Christ of the self-emptying (kenosis), of the divine power and attributes by the Son of God in the Incarnation, and of the Resurrection, who must be followed with infinite personal love and the greatest humility to the very end (Jn. 13:1); the only way to become like to the image of the Son . . . first-born of many brothers (Rom. 8:29). This image of Christ the man inspired Fr Arrupe in all his interventions at the International Congress of former Students in Valencia (1974), interventions which impressed profoundly a wide circle of the assembly and readers: 'It must be emphasized that the radical novelty of the Gospel lies in proclaiming this singular humanism, this new pattern of man, born out of his faith in Jesus: the man dead to all forms of egoism and later reborn from above, free to love, free to give life itself, free to commit himself completely to the service of others. . . . The man who finally, wholly intergrates within himself in faith and love, love of God and love for his fellow men; makes sincere and visible the social fecundity of our faith in Jesus, and thus assimilates Jesus, the man, to all other men'. (1-7-73).

It is the Christ of personal friendship, of trusting dialogue (Cf. the various texts of prayers written by Father General), of hope, ('Jesus Christ our hope,' 1 Tim. 1:1): 'Young people should be induced to nourish habitually a real and fraternal dialogue with Christ, always alive to the sufferings and aspirations of man, in all times of crisis, in the on-going history of the Church. It is appropriately he who personally talks to us and invites us to share with him the cross and the glory of saving mankind' (AR XV 115).

It is the Christ who lives and acts in a special way through his Vicar. In the closing Homily of the 32nd General Congregation, during the Concelebration in the Basilica of Saint Peter (6-3-75) after emphasizing the 'ecclesiastical transformation' of Ignatius of Loyola which drew him to his peculiar 'devotion' to the Pope, the General concluded: 'For Ignatius, from then onwards, the new criterion "to help souls" would be in relation to the Pope. "He was convinced", writes Nadal, "that Christ would deign to guide him along his path to the divine service through the Pope" (MN 1, 264). In the mystic life of Ignatius, the Roman Pontiff would from day to day appear more clearly as Christ's Vicar, and the complete and absolute consecration of Ignatius and his companions to the Eternal Father would in the future become a total availability to Christ's Vicar on earth. . .'

It is to the Christ of the Eucharist that Father General has more recently addressed himself publicly: 'To me the dialogue of intimate conversation with you, who are really present in the Eucharist and await me in the Tabernacle, has always been and still is a fountain of inspiration and strength: without these I could not continue, and much less be able to bear the weight of my responsibilities. The Mass, the Holy Sacrifice is the hub of my life. I cannot conceive of a single day without the celebration of or participation in the Eucharistic Sacrifice. Without the Mass my life would be empty, I would lack all strength; I feel this profoundly and so affirm it positively.'

The Vision of La Storta
It is impossible to end this brief sketch without simply mentioning another personal experience. Re-reading these writings of the Father General, I seem to have understood — at least partly — the innermost reason for his continuous reference to the vision of La Storta. It simply has to do with the 'image' of a Christ which subsumes or encompasses the whole Christ personally experienced. He tries to connect this Christ with all his personal experiences in his following of Jesus, which he wished would also be the case with all of us and with the Society. On the occasion of the renewal of the consecration of the Society to the Sacred Heart of Jesus (9-6-72) he placed himself (and tried to unite the whole Society of Jesus with him inside the tiny chapel of La Storta) in the very centre of that experience which summed up so many similar experiences of St Ignatius. For here stands the Trinitarian Christ, Son and Envoy, the union of God and the mission, the *kenosis* of the *Vexillum Crucis,* the realism of the following of Christ to Rome

under his Vicar, here the Christ of Hope, of the Paschal Mystery, 'If anyone will follow me . . .'.

This image of a Christ mysteriously unified in himself as God and man, in which the full mission and wishes of the Father are lived as such, and the wishes of the Father really become a mission, act as a magnet for Ignatius of Loyola and constitute in him the unifying centre of 'a contemplative in action' according to Nadal's definition.

This image — to judge by what he writes and says — today continues to attract Father General. His unifying purpose in the following of Jesus, in a way that 'union with God' and the 'mission' form an indestructible union, constitutes the fundamental nucleus of his letter of the 1 November 1981 to the whole Society, is easily identifiable in his writings.

'Let us keep the principle intact: the one that opens itself outwards, must no less open inwards, that is towards Christ. He who has to go to greater lengths to serve human needs, let him speak more intimately with Christ. He who has to be contemplative in his action let him endeavour to find in the intensification of his activities, the urgency for an intense contemplation. If we want to unfold to the world, we should do it like Christ, in such a way that our testimony springs forth, like his, from his way of life and his doctrine. Let us not fear becoming like him, a focus of contradiction and scandal. . . After all, not even he was understood by many. . .'

'Thus I wrote in 1977. I now ratify this. It relates to a Christ completely given to the love of the Father and, for that reason, oblivious of himself, given entirely to man.'

This deep love for man in the heart of God, which is the 'so much did God love mankind'. . ., has its theological locus and complete entity in the Heart of Jesus; wherein he loves those for which he exists, lives, acts and dies. And where every human being, accepting his love, discovers his personal reason for living and working, his centre, on which he can be re-formed in accordance with God's original project as man or woman for Christ and for all his brothers.

Fr Peter Arrupe has thus made of his life an adventure. He has progressively centred his life on this belief, simplifying it, and has

133

built his work on it. The preceding texts show us this — his secret.

As the Apostle John in his old age, feeble-mindedly repeated the *Amaos!*, so this veteran warrior and apostle, today physically handicapped, has tried to gather and summarize in these pages his 'motive' and to go with us in his own personal way to the core of the Gospel. We conclude with respect and with the conviction of having entered (or at least having glimpsed, thanks to him) the depths of that sanctuary of God, from where Christ renews everything, simplifies everything, gives everything, and is all in all — his Heart.

Ignatius Iglesias, S.J.
Madrid, 9th September 1982.